VOICES FROM
THE KITCHEN

VOICES FROM THE KITCHEN

PERSONAL NARRATIVES FROM NEW YORK'S IMMIGRANT RESTAURANT WORKERS

EDITED BY **MARC MEYER**

BEACON PRESS, BOSTON

BEACON PRESS
24 Farnsworth Street
Boston, Massachusetts 02110
www.beacon.org

Beacon Press books
are published under the auspices of
the Unitarian Universalist Association of Congregations.

28 27 26 25   8 7 6 5 4 3 2 1

This book is printed on acid-free paper that meets the uncoated paper
ANSI/NISO specifications for permanence as revised in 1992.

Text design and composition by Kim Arney

Some narrators' names have been changed in
the manuscript to protect their privacy.

*Library of Congress Cataloging-in-Publication
Data is available for this title.*
ISBN: 978-0-8070-2064-7; e-book: 978-0-8070-2065-4;
audiobook: 978-0-8070-2234-4

The authorized representative in the EU for product safety and
compliance is Easy Access System Europe 16879218, Mustamäe tee 50,
10621 Tallinn, Estonia: http://beacon.org/eu-contact.

To Vico (Virgilo) Ortega,
who lived his dream

CONTENTS

Preface • ix

VICO • 1

FANY • 9

ERNESTO • 19

ARMANDO • 25

ALONSO • 31

LUCIA • 39

LIGORIO • 45

DIANA • 53

MAMADOU • 59

JOSÉ • 63

CARLHA • 69

MOHAMMED • 77

JAKELINE • 83

ISLAM • 95

ROSIE • 103

MASSOUD • 111

JENNY • 121

ÁNGEL • 133

DIEGO · 141

VLAD · 149

JAIRO · 157

ONIKA · 163

DALILA · 175

ANGEL V. · 183

MOUSTAFA · 191

LUIS · 197

ANNA MARIE · 205

Acknowledgments · 223

PREFACE

Restaurants as we know them in the United States would not exist without immigrant labor. We would not be able to build them, staff them, or produce the food we serve without the people who have come to this country from other nations. When you are captivated by a delicious meal, even a slice of pizza on the street, know that there are compelling individuals in the background—all working together, learning the necessary tasks to expertly serve hundreds of customers from flaming burners or hot ovens. They come from Mexico, Bangladesh, Ecuador, Burkina Faso, and many other places. While diners celebrate special occasions around festive tables, there are unsung professionals working hard behind the scenes, usually with little recognition and certainly without accolades.

Along with my four business partners—Vicki Freeman, Chris Paraskevaides, Anna Marie McCullagh, and Ayesha Nurdjaja—I run a collection of New York City restaurants called the Bowery Group. The group includes Cookshop, Shuka, Vic's, Shukette, and Rosie's. You will see these names come up throughout this book. We have never made the slightest distinction about where any of our employees have come from. The only thing that matters is that we all work together to make a living. In my decades in the restaurant business, I've come to deeply appreciate the challenging tasks involved in preparing and serving food to the public. Yet we who run the restaurants have done too little to acknowledge the accomplishments of our workforce.

I never set out to be a chef or a restaurant owner. My father was an Air Force officer for whom joining the military was an act of rebellion against his newly minted American parents, secular Jews from Odessa and Kyiv. They expected my father to become a highly educated professional. Joining the Army Air Corp (as the Air Force was referred to at that time) was severely beneath family expectations. His personal act of defiance turned our household into a group of vagabonds, always moving from one air base to another. Growing up, I made few lasting connections to places or people. By the time I was eighteen, I had attended fifteen schools. Certainly, that lifestyle affects people—in my case, my life became one of stumbling from one thing to another.

I dropped out of college, drove trucks, and worked processing king crab in the Aleutian Islands. Then I found my way to Berkeley, California. Still lacking any real goal other than paying my bills, I took on two part-time jobs. One was cleaning vegetables and washing pots in a small café; the other was as a kitchen helper in a Chinese restaurant where I had been befriended by the owners, a mother and son team. This tiny restaurant had been my dining room several times a week for a number of years—a bowl of noodle soup with everything in it cost a dollar at the time. Still, I worked these jobs without any sense of purpose.

Then I came across a cookbook—*Classic Italian Cook Book* by Marcella Hazan. It opened a door to a cuisine that I knew next to nothing about. I cooked my way through the entire book. Then, in a characteristically desultory decision, I moved to New York City, where I found an entry-level job as a salad cook at a restaurant named One Fifth. The kitchen was run by the Austrian chef Anton Linder. It was in that kitchen that I found a belief in hard work, which led to a greater understanding of something that is a source of pride and meaning around the world—cooking. And so my life in the kitchens of New York restaurants began.

There is no single explanation as to what has moved countless people to seek jobs in the restaurants of New York. Certainly, many possess a clear and passionate drive to become part of this vibrant industry. Some of us were social misfits, ill-suited for the conformities of the corporate world. Others sought to escape dangerous social conditions. All of us had something that we needed to leave behind—a need to hide, to escape, to break the patterns of the past. Whether fleeing plantation slavery, corrupt governments, or a violent society, people have historically come to New York seeking refuge. And within this city, the restaurant world has offered some small reason for optimism. Whether we worked in the kitchen or the dining room, the restaurant became not only a place that inspired hopes and dreams but also a vantage point from which to look at the world.

I have worked shoulder to shoulder with individuals who have witnessed famine and organized brutality. I have shared meals with those who have trekked across deserts and hidden in the bellies of tanker trucks. They were my compatriots in the kitchen, but for quite some time I knew little about them beyond their first names or the jobs they performed.

As my career progressed, I began to feel that being an accomplished chef had to involve more than making food that would garner praise for my culinary virtues. I also wanted my work to say something about the society we live in and how world events have affected the people I work with.

For many years, I've been captivated by the oral histories of Studs Terkel and Svetlana Alexievich. The stories that their books present range from the hard-edged to the emotional to the tragic. All reveal a history told by ordinary people rather than scholars. So I set out to compile a list of about thirty employees—servers, dishwashers, cooks, hosts, bussers—to interview about their lives. I ended up with twenty-seven narratives. Some of the narrators I have known for over twenty-five years. In the case of some Mexican colleagues, I have traveled with them to visit their hometowns and parents and extended family. All the people I talked to I view with deep respect and appreciation.

It is with profound gratitude and care that I present this collection of twenty-seven personal histories. My role is not to interpret these stories—I do not speak for the narrators. Rather, my goal is to make space for the voices we do not hear enough of and to amplify them with compassion. It was not necessary to pose many questions: once I began asking about family, country, neighborhood, or the compelling reasons that had brought them to the US, they just talked. My interviewing technique would probably be considered unsophisticated—we sat in busy restaurant dining rooms, or in quiet areas before the restaurant opened, or opposite each other in a prep kitchen after everyone else had left. Generally, I began all of the interviews in the same manner by asking about childhood, school, parents, siblings, food, and the circumstances that had forced them to make life-changing decisions to leave home, family, country, and—importantly—language.

Rarely was there any need to direct or encourage the narrator on. In fact, there were several instances when the speaker stopped, looked down, then back into my eyes, and said, "Let me tell you something"— followed by tearful accounts of difficult experiences that I had not expected to hear. I used the voice memo app on my iPhone to record the conversations. All of the interviews except two (Jenny and Jakeline) were conducted in English. Those two were conducted in Spanish by Ixtzel Arreola, a Mexican children's book author, midwife, and artist, in collaboration with her partner, Tino Hanekamp, a German author and screenwriter. Tino and Ixtzel conducted the two Spanish interviews via telephone from their home in southern Mexico. Tino was especially instrumental in seeing this project to fruition. He helped me fully see the relevance of documenting the many stories told by the individuals who work in New York City restaurants. This book would not exist without his aid and influence.

All of the interviews were transcribed as faithfully as possible. They have been very lightly edited for clarity and to omit filler words and repeated phrases.

I don't believe the narrators would have shared these intimate experiences unless they felt completely comfortable. Everyone seemed honored that I had taken an interest in them beyond the workplace. Although there is an employer-employee dynamic that must be acknowledged, I have never for an instant viewed myself as a savior. I began this project not knowing where it would lead. But once we started the interviews, I felt a profound sense of honor and privilege for the honesty and trust the narrators bestowed on me.

To protect the narrators' privacy, some of their names have been changed. All proceeds from this book will be distributed equally among the narrators, who have also retained legal ownership over their stories.

My hope is that readers will connect with the strength, creativity, humor, and humanity that is so vividly apparent across these pages and that they come away with a new appreciation for the essential contributions of this workforce. They have enabled me to share my culinary passion with the world. My obligation is to reciprocate through concrete actions that lift up these staff members who have lifted me up each day.

VOICES FROM THE KITCHEN

VICO

I'm from Mexico, from a village called Peña Colorada in the state of Puebla. Our village is so small, it doesn't exist on the map. It's a beautiful, beautiful village.

I lost my father when I was twelve years old. We were three brothers, four sisters, and my mother. After my father passed away, my mother opened a small grocery store in our house and started a bakery. I began baking at the age of thirteen. We were the only bakery in the area and made sweet bread and *bolillos*, all by hand. The oven was fired with wood.

We had a decent life—we always had food on the table—we just didn't have enough for me to go to college. The college was a three-hour drive away, and I would have had to rent a place, buy my own food, and so on. We just couldn't afford it. That's one of the three reasons I came to the United States when I was twenty-one.

After my father died, a friend of his said to me, "From now on, you're responsible for this family, and you will be forever." I always kept that in mind. And that's the second and main reason I left Mexico: to support my family and make money for college. I'm the oldest, so it was me who had to leave. So, after I finished high school and passed the tests to enter college, I said to my mom, "Let me go to the US for a year. Let me save some money and come back and start my studies." Well, that never happened. I stayed here, and with the money I made I helped my family. They got rid of the bakery, but they kept the store.

The third reason I left was that I was tired of making bread after doing it for almost ten years. I was ready for something new. Funny thing is, when I got here, I quickly realized that the only way to make decent money was by making bread. (*Laughs.*) That's how I started working in the kitchen again. And here I am.

I took a bus all the way up to Baja California and crossed from Tijuana to San Diego. At that time, you could just walk across the border. I crossed five times in the five years to come, because I used to go to Mexico every year to see my mom and siblings. Crossing was so easy back then. One time, Immigration caught me and the officer said, "Don't worry, just try again." I said, "Thank you, I will." And after a few hours, I did and made it. (*Laughs.*)

When you go to the United States, you go where you have family, and that's why I came to New York. I had my aunt here, my mom's sister. She lived in the neighborhood known as Barrio 16 on Third Avenue near 116th Street. Her apartment was on the sixth floor, and through one of the few windows, you could see an old, abandoned building where people were doing drugs and other things.

The first few weeks I didn't work and spent a lot of time looking through that window thinking, "Wow, what a life." (*Laughs.*) Yeah, it was kind of frustrating in the beginning. It took me a while to adjust. One of the biggest frustrations for me was the food. In those days, it was hard to find tortillas, jalapeños, cilantro, Mexican cheese, or even pig fat. They basically didn't exist. It was 1986.

My first job was as a porter in a restaurant called Betty Brown, near the corner of Houston and Broadway. I cleaned the kitchen, and the runners and bussers were making fun of me because I was so fast and running all the time. They said, "Oh, we're going to take a picture of you and give it to the boss so he can pay you more." But I wanted to make it. I wanted to prove that I could do the job. And I did—for three days. Then the restaurant closed. (*Laughs.*)

After that, I went to work at Ernie's. Then I came back because by then, the former owners of Betty Brown had opened the Big Kahuna. And that's basically when I started cooking. The Big Kahuna was a fun bar. There was a cover charge, and people got drunk like crazy. It was all about drinking. They only sold burgers, hot dogs, nachos, and things like that. That's the job they gave me. They put me in a food stall, where I had my tiny kitchen, my register, and that little window through which I gave the food to the customers.

I barely spoke English at that time, but I didn't really need it anyway because I was serving mostly drunk people. "Give me a hot dog!" "Give me a burger!" Well, how hard is that? (*Laughs.*) The main thing in that place was the bar. That's where they made the money. Nobody paid much attention to me. But it was there that I realized that working as a cook wasn't a bad idea.

From the Big Kahuna I went to Poiret, a French restaurant. And that's where I started making bread again, because the chef saw my abilities with dough and flour and taught me how to make pastry. I always tried not to stay too long at the same place and try new things. That's how I got deeper and deeper into cooking. When I was doing salads and there was nothing to do, I used to go to the line and help the cooks and learn.

My first dish was tuna *misol*. You put chunks of tuna in a pan, take them out, and add wine and capers, and so on. It's a tricky sauce to make because it often breaks when you finish it with butter and the pan is too hot. That was my challenge—and my first dish.

But primarily, I was doing salads and pastries. I worked at Poiret for five years, and I also worked at Bayamo, a Latin Asian restaurant by Stewart Rosen, where I did prep work. I always had two jobs back then. Later, I went to Mackinac, where I met you, and when I worked there, I also worked at Ferrari's. I always had these two jobs to save money and send it to my family.

The first five years I went to Mexico once a year. But then in 1991, I got married and soon after my daughter was born and I didn't go back to Mexico until 2003 because, you know, I didn't want to risk anything. I didn't go for thirteen years, until I got my papers.

[I've been] a citizen now for eight years. My daughter is thirty-one, has a master's in math, and teaches algebra in high school. My son is twenty-eight and an English teacher, also in high school. He once spent three years in Mexico.

One day he said to me, "I have to be in Michoacán on the fifth of February because I'm starting to work there." He had applied for a job teaching English in a private school in Zamora. My wife was very worried. It wasn't just that it was Mexico, but Michoacán, one of the worst states in terms of violence, drugs, and everything. And on top of that, our son was quite spoiled. By that time, I already had the restaurant, so he would just come and eat. He couldn't even fry an egg!

So, my wife was worried. I told her, "Don't worry about this *pendejo*"—excuse my language. "You will have him back by next week. He will not be able to make it down there!" But I was very wrong. The guy didn't come back for three years! He loved Mexico. (*Laughs.*) I mean, you think you know your kids . . .

After a year or so, I went there to see him because, from time to time, you have to take care of your kid, right? And what does this guy do? He tells me a story: "Father, do you remember when we passed that bridge the other day? Well, there is this rich kid who had that beautiful motorcycle. Yesterday they took the motorcycle and shot him there, just like that." That's the kind of story he told me!

Luckily, he never smoked or drank, so he didn't hang around with shady characters. Instead, he traveled! He went to all these beautiful towns, all these *pueblos mágicos*, and these travels and his life there changed him. When he came back after three years, he was a different person. He didn't waste food anymore, was very responsible and polite to people, and appreciated the life he had here more—a completely different man. Plus, now he knows more about Mexico than I do! (*Laughs.*)

My kids are my biggest achievement, my triumph. And that I was also successful in my work, well . . . It wasn't my idea to start my own business, it was my brother-in-law's. He wanted to open a grocery store, and I said, "If you really want to do it, make a café-slash-grocery, and we could sell baked goods there too." At that time, I was working at Columbus Bakery, and you remember the tiles they had on the walls, these broken plates and everything? I immediately started to break plates. (*Laughs.*) I just copied it, and that style was something unusual in our neighborhood. It took me eight months to open La Flor. And soon after, we had a line for, I think, the next five years. It was a great business.

I started living my life. I was learning how to enjoy it. And when you're in that business, your customers tell you what restaurants to go to, because that's what they do. They go from restaurant to restaurant.

So, they told me to go to March Restaurant and places like that, and I did. I went to March, Daniel, Le Bernardin, all these good, fine places. And if the dinner for my wife and me cost nine hundred bucks, who cares? I was making a lot of money at La Flor and was still working at Columbus Bakery.

We opened a second place, a taqueria, and it was also successful. Then my brother-in-law fell in love with one of the servers. The problem was, he was married and had a kid with his wife, and that whole situation started to create some issues in the family. Since we were partners, it involved me too. So, I said, "Listen, we have two places. Choose which one you want." He stayed with the taqueria, and I stayed with La Flor. Sadly, he lost his place. He lost everything.

I was doing well in those days, and I could have kept opening new restaurants on my own. But I also had kids to think about, and I always made sure to send them to Catholic schools, which were expensive. So, when people came to me and wanted to open restaurants with me, but only if I worked exclusively for them, it was a difficult decision. In the end, I decided to go with them because it was a secure arrangement. I chose to stay with the safe option, and the main reason was the education of my kids. That's why I got stuck working for others instead of growing for myself. But even if I had chosen to do my own projects, I couldn't be more successful than I am now. Still, sometimes I wonder what would have happened if I hadn't taken the safe route and gone my own way.

My restaurant La Flor has been open for twenty-three years now. I don't even know my official position there. (*Laughs.*) I think I'm the executive chef. I oversee twenty-two restaurants that belong to the company I work for. I write the menus for most of them, and they are all doing well. I don't know if I'm just lucky or . . . I mean, it's all about finding the right people, right? And by "right people," I mean good chefs. If the chef is good, the restaurant will do well, and I'm happy.

My biggest headaches are with Sequoia because it's a seasonal restaurant. Every year we need to hire people, fire them, and then hire again. And the way things are these days, it's not easy. Even a young person who just came from Guatemala can sue you if you don't do the right thing. They know the law, and they'll take you to court. It's crazy.

I miss the old days when people were loyal. They really wanted to prove themselves. All they needed was an opportunity, and they would take it and run with it. Nowadays, you give someone an opportunity, and . . . (*Throws hands up.*)

My cooking roots are of course in my mother's cooking at home in our little village, Peña Colorada. My mother used to make her dishes from scratch with just six or seven ingredients. She only used what she needed and never wasted anything. I guess that's where I learned to appreciate the flavors and to appreciate food.

In those days, we didn't have gas. We cooked with wood. When we finished cooking and the wood was still glowing, we used that heat to warm tortillas. You didn't need to put anything on the tortilla, maybe a little salt. That was it. The flavor was amazing. When these memories come back, they make me do crazy things in restaurant kitchens here. I try to recreate that taste, that moment, that memory.

Another thing is the ingredients. The corn down there is completely different from the corn here. It has flavor! And the tomatoes, the meat, at least back then . . . You didn't need to put sauce on the meat. Here, if you don't put a sauce on the meat, it's like eating cardboard.

Mothers in those days saved everything. They never wasted anything. For example, they would use vanilla beans, the seeds and pods, multiple times because the flavor was still there. They always tried to get the most out of everything.

Back then in my time, they grew mostly watermelons, melons, corn, peanuts, and sesame in our area. But there are some wild fruits that people ate sometimes because they didn't have anything else. They are delicious and are starting to come here too, fruits like *mamey*, *jiotilla*, and guava.

Something else I realized while living here: People there, back in the day, never got sick or went to doctors or had surgeries. They died because they were eighty or ninety years old. Another person died because they were killed or had an accident, things like that. But you never heard of someone losing a leg because of diabetes. These things didn't exist back then. But now, it's a completely different story. And I really believe it's because of what we're eating, the things we put in our bodies.

The immense health problems in Mexico nowadays—it's the fast food, the Coca-Cola, but most of all the lack of education. And the meat these days! My brother and I, we have a farm down there, at least we're trying. We have cows, and we're trying to make them gain weight so we can sell them, but it's hard when you want to do the right thing and just feed corn and grass or things like that. So, we went to other farms to see how they do it, and when you are aware of that reality, you don't want to eat meat anymore. What they feed their cows—chicken shit and all kinds of waste—you cannot even eat the intestines anymore; they are so damaged. It's really bad.

But that's what everybody is doing right now. And trying to raise your cows the natural way, you just can't compete. I will keep on doing it, but just for my family. I just try to take care of my family and teach my kids what to eat and what not. In the end, it's going to be their lives, and I want it to be good. That's my main reason for everything: I want them to have a better life than me. More happiness. If I don't do it, I don't think anybody else is going to do it for them.

FANY

I'm from Honduras, from a town called Juticalpa in the center of the country. I was born into a big Catholic family that liked to eat, dance, and party. I have two brothers and one sister. I'm the second oldest and *the* adult. (*Laughs.*) I was raised by my grandma, the head of the family.

My mom was always working to support the family; I rarely saw her. She worked for one of the richest families in our city. They owned a lot of businesses, like gas stations, pharmacies, and restaurants. Officially, my mom was the administrator, but she was more like a manager and basically did everything. We usually saw her only twice a month, when she came by to bring money and sign papers for school and other things.

My father had left us when I was four and my sister was just a baby. He was a musician and played with his band in the only dance club in town. My mother's family never liked him, which made it extra hard for my mother. At some point he started going to countries like Panama looking for job opportunities. Meanwhile, we moved into my grandmother's house: my three siblings, my mother, and me. And that's where I grew up, because my father—he simply didn't come back. Later we learned that he had become a coyote, which was very dishonorable. We were not allowed to talk about him anymore.

My grandmother's house was enormous and more than a hundred years old, with high ceilings and a big garden. It was always full of life because we were many—my siblings, my aunt and her daughter, and a couple of young people my grandmother was renting rooms to. Growing up there was great. And I knew how to have fun. I'm a little bit naughty, you know. (*Laughs.*) I always had a lot of energy. I broke my leg, my arm, and always found a way to get in trouble.

Our family is a really old family. We didn't have much money, but we had a name. My grandma always told me, "Listen, sometimes you don't need money, you just need your work." It's about honor, and it's about legacy. If you come from an old family with an honorable name, and when people know that there was no corruption in your family, no criminal business, they respect you. Since I was little, I knew that there was clean and dirty. Our last two presidents were almost our neighbors, and one block around the corner lived one of the oldest mafia leaders we had. We were raised to be polite, but we knew what he was doing, and people like him got respected out of fear. We got respected out of honor.

The best part of my childhood was my grandmother's food. She was a fantastic cook. She could make wonderful dishes just with salt, pepper, garlic, and some herbs from the garden. Anything else—all these fancy things we have now, like consommé, sauce, and exotic spices—didn't exist for her. She cooked for every occasion. If we were sad or there was a celebration, she would cook the right thing. And if somebody didn't like a certain kind of food, she would cook something else just for him or her. She would cook three different meals, just to make everybody happy.

She was a little bit military, though. If she said dinner time was seven o'clock, you better be there at seven o'clock—ready, clean, and always with shoes on. Also, the moment we got up in the morning we had to shower and dress properly. We had to be presentable because we had a name.

I did great in school, and I was famous because I made everybody laugh and had friends everywhere. Everybody knew me! (*Laughs.*) I went to elementary, middle, and high school, and then I went to college. In high school I was the president of my class and several social and church clubs—I was the president everywhere. (*Laughs.*)

I was raised with strong Catholic principles, and from childhood days on I was a ministrant. It was fun, I enjoyed it, and I always believed in God. It's just the way they see Him, how they think about Him, that didn't always seem correct to me. Something was wrong, I always thought that. God can't be like that. I questioned that from when I was little. That got me a lot from above (*makes beating gestures*) from my

grandma. But I got in trouble anyway because I even questioned political life, the economy, and so on. I was that little one who questioned
everything! (*Laughs.*)

I always had the feeling that God brought me here for a reason, and
I needed to find it. My grandma and my mom hoped that when I grew
up, I would get married and have children, and that would be it. But
I also think they sensed that I was gay since I was little. That's why
they were stricter with me, and I think that's why I was questioning
everything, because of that dynamic. Now, looking back, I feel sorry
for my grandma. I gave her a hard time. Plus, this attitude always got
me into some kind of trouble, at every stage of my life. But the truth
is, I question everything because I want to know everything! (*Laughs.*)

I [had gone] to university for almost three years when I had to start
working. It was a turbulent time because I was in my first real relationship with a woman, and my family didn't want to support me anymore.
So, I had to work. My first job was for the municipality, where I realized
how easily people can be embarrassed and humiliated by bureaucracy
because of the way it is designed and the people who are in power. Then
I started working for an NGO in the capital that helped women with
programs for childbirth, economics, and education—women who could
not read, had never gone to school, lived in very rural areas, and had
very few opportunities. That's how it began.

I started to see my country from another perspective. I always knew
that Honduran society was not fair. I knew about the inequality and
the corruption and criminality and all that, but now I felt deep shame.
I tried to help, but I saw all these people dying anyway, of hunger or
whatever, and I asked myself, "How can this be? How can we let this
happen?" Something inside of me changed. I feel so much love for my
country, I really do. And I don't know why, but I always believed that
I could be the person to change something, make a little difference.

So, when one of my aunts contacted me and offered me a job for
another NGO called CIPE [the Center for International Private Enter-
prise], I happily accepted and threw myself into the work. That job was
very important to me; it really marked my heart. I could use all my skills
and energy and found ways to reach people. It's the story of my life.

I was sent to the Lenca, the Indigenous people of my country, who live in the southeast in the highlands, far away from the cities. I was visiting every single family, every single home, sometimes walking eight hours to get from one house to another. It was awesome. Back then, these people weren't even part of society and lived in great poverty. Once a year a helicopter from the government came and dropped some food, and that was it. My job was to inform them about the possibilities of support and to generally help them.

There I realized that education is everything. If you don't educate people, they don't realize that they can do a lot with the little they have. So, I brought programs about agriculture and education. For example, I taught them about the fruits and vegetables they could grow. They were planting things, but they didn't know how to be sustainable. Almost all they grew were potatoes. Where they live, it's raining all the time, it's really cold and wet and super high, and they didn't realize they could cultivate many other crops too, so we brought them seeds and taught them methods. I lived with them for more than a year. It was a beautiful job.

Then the organization sent me to another part of the country, to Santa Barbara, to the jungle people, because there was a lot of violence. It was the time when all these Colombian and Mexican influences got into my country. It was as if a bomb had exploded—suddenly everybody wanted to be a narco. So, my NGO started a program for young people from broken homes and bad neighborhoods, and my job was to go to the areas with the highest narco activities and find these kids, talk to them, and find out what they needed to live a life without violence and drugs.

The problem in countries like mine is always structural. Everything is run by groups, so I always had to understand the hierarchy first. I had to find the leader, talk to him, get permission to go on, and like that I got access and found the kids that needed help—kids that were white-skinned and blue-eyed, by the way, as are most people who live in that area. I did interview after interview, made the project, presented it to my organization, they gave the funds, and I got started.

It was very successful. We had a huge campaign called Young People for Peace. Even TV reporters came to town. We wanted to catch the government's attention so we could apply for programs to give those young people different opportunities. Some people are not good at school and don't want to study, but if you give them the right program, they can become a cook, maybe a great cook, or a carpenter or a nurse. But back then, all this education cost money, money that you had to pay for yourself. The government wasn't supporting anything. That's where we stepped in. This is what we wanted to change, and not only for young people. In the end, it's all about education. Education can change everything, no matter how old you are.

I left my country because I fell in love. The person I fell in love with—now my wife—lived in New York and was too scared to come to my country, which is also her country. She is also from Honduras, from my city, but I met her on Facebook—can you believe it? (*Laughs.*) That's a good story. We are the 1 percent of people for whom meeting on Facebook was a good story. Because I was working for an NGO in my country, I had traveled a lot to countries like Guatemala and El Salvador, so it was easier for me to get a visa. But mostly I talked my way into it. (*Laughs.*) And that's why I came to the US by airplane. It was my first time on a plane.

I left my country because of love, but I had already known before I met Dalila,* my wife, that I would have to leave. The violence had gotten very bad and was reaching deeper and deeper. And when you do the kind of work I did, you get to meet the faces of corruption, which is dangerous enough. But I was always someone who spoke my mind—I couldn't help it, I'm a rebel. (*Laughs.*) And I did things the correct and honest way, and people didn't like it and gave me a lot of trouble. It's corruption, plain and simple. Leaders ask for help for their people, and then they give them only the least and keep the rest for themselves. I felt the heat rising, even inside the NGO, and sooner or later, all of that would have gotten me killed. So, I knew I had to leave my country. And when I met this woman on Facebook and she started talking about all the opportunities she had in the US, that you can really make it here if you work hard. . . . (*Laughs.*)

---

* See Dalila's story on page 175.

I want to be honest with you: I always saw the United States as a slave country, a country full of modern slaves. And I really didn't want to be there. Because the people who leave my country, they never come back. And when they do, they just die. I always asked myself, "Why do they never come back?" With the money they made in the United States, they could build a house in Honduras, open a business, and so on. But they don't come back, or they do when they are way too old. To me, that was a form of slavery—they were enslaved to whatever they were doing in the United States, and now they couldn't come back. That was my thinking. Thank God Dalila brought me here—that changed my mind. (*Laughs.*)

When I got here, I was no longer young, and my wife said, "You must forget who you are. Here, you are nobody. The first thing you are going to do is clean bathrooms." She always tells me the truth! (*Laughs.*) I said, "No problem, I can do that." And that was the first job I got here, cleaning houses. But not in New York, but in Virginia, where my brother lived.

I mean, I had met that woman [Dalila] for the first time when she picked me up at LaGuardia. We spent three days together, but I didn't know if the relationship would work, and I needed to make some money. And since I didn't know anybody in New York, I went to Virginia, where my brother got me a job at a cleaning company. On my first day, I started working at 7 a.m., and they brought us to this house, the most gorgeous and beautiful house I had ever seen in my life. We cleaned houses for people who were incredibly wealthy. I did that for one month, and then I went back to New York, where I rented a tiny apartment with just a tiny bed. The cleaning was better there. I love New York. I'll tell you something: *I love New York!* (*Laughs.*) This is my second home. I'm here, 100 percent.

New York can be wild, savage, like a jungle. But it gives you a lot of opportunities. For work, and for figuring out what you really want to do with your life, this is the place. Maybe not for raising kids, though. But for really living and doing your thing, this is the city.

I hated cleaning because I cleaned for people who were really picky and cheap. But I was really good at it because if I do something, I do it right. I was really organized and cleaned even parts that nobody saw or checked, but that took me longer and the money wasn't enough. So, listen to this: There was this one house we were cleaning, a huge house with elevators. The owner was a Russian Jewish guy named Mr. Salomon, a nice person. He had some kind of construction company, and one day he asked me if I knew someone who could work for him. He needed a construction worker. I said, "Does it have to be a man?" He said, "I don't care what it is, I just want someone who wants to work." I said, "Me! Take me! I don't like cleaning, but I like a good weekly salary." He said, "OK, I'll take you. A lot of my friends will be angry with me because if they have a good cleaning lady, they don't want to lose her. Now they'll lose you, but you'll still clean for me. The only house you'll clean is mine." I said, "OK, it's a deal." So, I started working in construction.

First, I just picked up things from demolitions, debris, and rubble. Then I got curious and wanted to learn, so I started cutting wood, sanding, framing, and all kinds of other things. I was in construction for almost three years! Then I got sick, one guy got caught*, Mr. Salomon had to close the company and . . . Well, there were many things happening at the same time, but the bottom line was that I couldn't work in construction anymore because my body was compromised. I still needed to work, though. My wife and I were in a tight financial situation. We didn't even have enough money for a MetroCard!

So, a friend of mine brought me to Long Island City, to a cookie factory called Eleni's. They make really fancy, beautiful cookies there. The manager, a gringo man but nice, I'll never forget him, said, "I want to hire you guys. But you have to teach me. I need a cleaning plan, because I don't know how to do it." It was a factory and very busy. I said, "Don't worry, Mr. Eddie. We'll clean this factory, and we'll figure out how to do it the best! Just let us do it." And so, we did, just the two of us, my friend and I, cleaning the whole cookie factory. They liked our work a lot.

---

* Most of the workers were undocumented.

And I saw the machine they used to make the dough, the ladies punching the cookies, and all these things, and I got curious. So, we cleaned, and we were fast and got faster, extra fast, so we had time left, and in that time we helped the ladies, and I learned how to punch the cookies and how to put the dough in the machine. After a year, I was the number one at doing those things, the best and the fastest! (*Laughs.*)

We spent a year at Eleni's, then the factory closed. But I had made a friend there, a Mexican woman named Lucrecia. I will never forget her either. She had a friend from Mexico who was a chef at an Italian restaurant in the West Village called Lil' Frankie's. Lucrecia said to me, "Fany, go there, ask for the chef, and tell him I sent you." They needed a dishwasher. The chef asked, "Do you have a problem with that?" I said, "I don't have a problem with being anything. You can give me any job as long as you teach me how to do it. And I will learn quickly." They told me that I would also have to take care of the garbage. I said, "Don't worry, I've got it."

It was a very busy place, and everything was really fast. I liked it. In my second or third week there, the chef said to me, "Hey, Fany, do you want to learn how to prep the pasta station?" I said, "Yes, I can do that. But only if you give me more money." He said, "Yeah, okay. What do you make now?" I was making ten dollars per hour. He said, "I'll give you one more dollar." I said, "OK." So, I prepped the pasta station. Soon, they let me prep all the stations in the kitchen for the chefs at night, so I had to make the salsas and do all the prep work. I said to the chef, "If you want to give me more money, that would be great. Because what I'm doing now comes with more responsibility." So, he gave me a raise to twelve dollars per hour.

Then he saw how I was doing. This place, you know, was narrow, and I had to bring all the salsas to where they were working and so on—it was crazy, but I liked it. After some time, the chef said, "Hey, Fany, can you also do the prep for the pizza station?" I said, "Will you give me more money?" He said, "Yes, and more hours!" So, they gave me a raise. (*Laughs.*) Another dollar. And I started working extremely long days. It was wild, it was wonderful, and it was a lot of money.

I did this for a while, and then the chef came to me. "Fany, I need to talk to you." I said, "Yes, chef. What is it?" He said, "Listen, this is going to change everything. The garde-manger* lady is pregnant, so do you want to do the salads? Would you like to be the garde-manger chef?" I said, "Yes, yes! But listen, chef, I've never cooked in my life, especially not Italian food with all these ingredients I don't even know the names of." He said, "Don't worry, we'll teach and train you." I said, "OK, if you think I can do it and if you give me more money, no problem." (*Laughs.*)

In the kitchen, I fell in love. Even before that, if I was cleaning or taking out the garbage, I always tried to find the passion in it, because whatever you do, if you do it with love, you will feel more at ease, more comfortable, and happier. So, I had this good attitude all the time because I believe that what you give, you will get back. But now I was cooking, and it was easy to fall in love with that. The vegetables alone! Ever since I was a kid, I always loved vegetables. I was that baby who took a bite of an onion! (*Laughs.*) And back then when I lived in my grandmother's house, I always loved to watch her cook. So, when they put me to work in the kitchen at Lil' Frankie's, I was hooked. I completely fell in love with cooking. And of course, it made me think of home and my grandmother.

My grandmother passed away two years ago during the pandemic. Everything she cooked was so simple, but the flavors she created were impressive and mysterious. Just her rice! She didn't put anything in it, just a little bit of oil, some salt in the oil, a little bit of pepper, and onion, but in tiny pieces that you couldn't even see because she didn't like seeing onions in the rice. She was old-school. And the way she cooked meat! The *bistec*, the beef—she didn't use tomato paste. She took the tomatoes and grated them, then added onions, pepper, salt, and garlic. It was divine. She had a system for creating flavor that was unique and simple. That's what I love.

---

* *Garde-manger*: Generally refers to the preparation of cold foods. In a restaurant kitchen, it usually refers to the salad station.

One of my favorite dishes is Honduran *tapado*. You put different kinds of meat, like beef, ribs, chorizo, and pork belly, and add pepper and onion, along with a lot of other juicy ingredients. Season it, then add plantain, potato, yucca, and green bananas. Cover it with a plantain leaf and let it all cook for three hours on a fire made in the ground. It tastes delicious! And the beans we have over there!

So, I fell in love with cooking. But at Lil' Frankie's, I was working too much. My wife and I have a daughter who is seventeen—she is from my wife's previous relationship, but now she is ours, and she and my wife were saying, "We never see you anymore," and so on, you know? (*Laughs.*) So, I looked for another job with fewer hours and the same pay. I worked at different places over the years, learned a lot, and then I arrived here.

I'm forty years old. My wife and I have been together for eleven years and we got married last year. I have a little dog named Benjamin Franklin. I miss my grandmother. My mother is alive and doing well. My father died alone while his new wife was in prison. I'm happy here. Our daughter just finished high school, and we are very proud. I've met so many wonderful people along the way and I've made so many friends. I make friends everywhere! (*Laughs.*)

ERNESTO

I am from La Venta [Mexico], a tiny town with 250 inhabitants, an hour and a half from Puebla. My father planted limes, peanuts, corn, watermelons, beans, onions, and *nardos*, a flower with a long stem and tiny white, very aromatic flowers. Sometimes buyers came and bought the good stuff directly from the field, the big limes or onions, but most of his produce my father sold at the market in Atlixco, a city thirty-five minutes from our town.

I never went to bed with an empty stomach. My father always did whatever he could to support his family and took me to the fields since I was very little so I wouldn't mess around the house. (*Laughs.*) I just sat there and played with the ants or built roads for my toy cars. When I was seven, I started helping him and my two older brothers. A few years later, my oldest brother went to New York, and a few years after that, my other brother followed, and I was the only son left and my father's right hand.

My father was always a farmer. As a teenager, his father wanted to take him to Mexico City, but my father was scared and let the opportunity pass. He chose to stay. I didn't. I left when I was fifteen, to New York, like my brothers.

Things had changed three years before, with the devaluation of the peso at the end of 1994. Times had gotten harder. We still had our land, but my father struggled a lot. To keep up with everything, he had to invest, and to invest, he had to borrow money and pay it back with high interest, and invest again and so on—it's a circle that never ends. Another problem was water. My town is small and there was never as much water as in the other towns. The other towns had the river, but we didn't have the river and no *ojo de agua*,* no spring, so when there were no rains, between October and early May, it was a dry town.

I'd never left our country before. My parents didn't like the idea of me going to New York or anywhere. It was hard for them to let me go because I was so young. It wasn't easy for me either. The hardest part was saying goodbye to my grandmother. The most wonderful times of my childhood I had with her. And how I loved her cooking—oh, how she cooked! How she prepared all this simple food that was so delicious!

She always had something to feed the family with, always something to give to us, even if it just was a fried egg with onions and jalapeños. One of my favorite dishes were her corn dough balls filled with *chile guajillo*, served with spicy tomato sauce and *epazote*, and at the end, she would just sprinkle some *queso fresco* or *queso añejo* on top and some onions.

And how I loved her mole! She cooked it in a huge *cazuela*, a ceramic casserole. In my family, everybody has their own way of making the mole, but my grandma's was always the best—just the right balance between sweet and spicy and this incredible richness. I don't know how she did it but maybe buying the ingredients was already part of the magic. One week she went to the market to buy the chilies; the next week she would get the seeds, then the chocolate and the cinnamon, and so on. I remember her being on her knees in the kitchen and grinding the seeds with the *metate*. She did everything by hand until she was too old. When I left, I knew I would never see her again.

We crossed the border in Sonora—a small group, twelve people, all from the same town and almost all of them my age, just kids really. We started walking by night; you always start at night. It took us three nights and two days. It's like an adventure, like in the old movies, the westerns—you are walking over hills, through the dry land, you are in danger, they might get you, there are cacti shaped like humans raising their hands, it's hot during the day and cold at night. I carried two gallons of water, canned food, tuna and cookies, nothing fancy. We told

---

* *Ojo de agua*: an idiom for a source of water, such as a well or spring.

each other stories about our old life in Mexico and what we hoped for our new life, the one ahead of us.

When I came to New York, my oldest brother asked me, "What do you want to do? There are no fields here and what else do you know?" I said, "I want to be a cook." I thought I could start working in a restaurant as a dishwasher and then learn how to cook. The problem was, I had a baby face. I really looked like the fifteen years I was and simply couldn't lie about my age and pretend to be eighteen. (*Laughs.*) So, I moved to New Jersey where I lived with one of my aunts, worked in a factory, and watched cartoons with the boy she was babysitting. And that's how I learned English.

A year later I moved back to New York, into an apartment in the Bronx with my brother. My first restaurant job was in a Chinese fast-food place on 103rd Street and 2nd Avenue, close to the Metropolitan Hospital. I was cutting vegetables and chicken and made sure the working stations were prepared and everything was clean. The job started at ten in the morning and ended at 11:30 at night with a twenty-minute lunch break at four. I stayed there for five months and then I went to a Japanese restaurant on 72nd and Columbus, where I made tempura.

A guy my age was working on the line there and started to teach me how to cook Japanese. That's how I learned that there is a difference between *yakisoba* and *yakiudon*. (*Laughs.*) The head chef was from Ecuador and [had] worked there since 1980. He had started as a dishwasher and had learned everything he knew from the old head chef, a very old Japanese [man]. And now I learned everything from him; his name was Angel. The second in command was from Puebla, two other coworkers were from Guerrero, and they'd all worked there a long time, and the menu never changed.

I will never forget how they made their teriyaki sauce. At the end of every week, they put this huge pile of chicken bones in a big pot with water, left it there overnight, and that's how they produced the stock. The next morning, we strained it and added the soy sauce and all the ingredients, but the base was this stock. A lot of labor, but the flavor was incredible—I never tasted teriyaki sauce like this. And with this sauce, I fell in love with cooking. I saw how they did it, that it wasn't that complicated, and I thought, I can do it too. Unfortunately, they had to close the restaurant and move to a place that was too small for all the staff, so they let me go.

I found work as a salad guy in a Mexican restaurant called Red at Fulton Street. The food wasn't very sophisticated, but the place was big and busy, and the first day I got into the line behind the salad station I was shaking. All I was hearing was Caesar salad, Caesar chicken, Caesar, Caesar, Caesar! (*Laughs*.) But soon I was watching the other guys and what they were doing at the grill and the other stations. They said, "You wanna learn?" Of course I wanted to. And so, they taught me. I was there for five years until one of the guys started working at a fine restaurant at 11th Street and Washington and told me he had a place for me there.

It was an Italian restaurant named Avanti, and it had a Michelin star, but it wasn't for me. All the *mise en place** you had to make each day. Every day you had to start from scratch! That's when I realized that my heart was with the simple cooking of my grandmother. Luckily, the owners had another, more casual restaurant with a small kitchen, a small team, and only four dishes: fish, schnitzel, chicken, beef. I loved this place and stayed there for seven years until I was twenty-five and longed to learn more. So, I read menus of restaurants until I found one that sounded interesting: a French restaurant called Le Zoo. There I realized that French cuisine was my thing. I wanted to learn all about it. And that's what I did. But my grandmother's cooking, her food, and the simple way she prepared it, never left me.

In her kitchen were a few things that always had to be there: *maiz*, beans, chilies, firewood, and the three essential tools of Mexican cooking—the *molcajete*, the *metate*, and the *comal*.** With these three tools she made everything.

Like the *salsa macha*: just roasted chilies—any kind of chilies, jalapeño, habanero or poblano—and you roast them with garlic and sea

---

* *Mise en place*: a French term that refers to preparing a dish's ingredients at a cook's station before cooking.
** *Molcajete*: a stone mortar and pestle. *Metate*: a curved oblong stone and a smaller stone used for grinding grains, corn, cocoa, or seeds. *Comal*: a round flat griddle made of stone or steel, generally heated with a wood fire or propane burner.

salt and mash it all with the *molcajete*. For the roasting, she always used the *comal* that was still hot after the tortillas were prepared. And that's also how she roasted the tomatoes for the *salsa roja* and the dried chilies for the *salsa adobo*. It all went on the *comal* and after that into the *molcajete*.

One of my favorite dishes was *frijoles quebrados*, broken beans. My grandmother crushed black beans with the *metate*, washed them to take the peels off, and then boiled them with onions, garlic, and *epazote*— simple and delicious. As was her *hígado de pollo*, her chicken liver. She just cleaned and sliced the livers, cooked them with onion and jalapeño, added some *hierbabuena*—and there you'd have your delicious taco.

Another favorite was *tamal de cominos*. She put the masa in a bowl, added salt, cumin, *epazote*, and *chile guajillo*, rolled it all up, threw it in boiling water, almost like gnocchi, and served it with an adobo-like salsa. That was a dish we would eat when the weather was very cold or on one of these days when you wake up and it's still raining.

Sometimes she made eggs from inside a hen. You know, when the hen is killed, before the eggs are laid? To make the broth my grandmother only used water, onion, garlic, and *hierbabuena*, and she'd let the egg bulbs scooped out of the hen boil with it. The first time I saw it as a child, I found it very scary because I had never seen eggs without their shell like this before, but, well, it was very tasty. (*Laughs.*)

And then there was her *tamal de axolote* . . . You know these sala- manders who live in the water? She grabbed the salamander and cleaned it, added some *epazote* and salt, wrapped it in an *hoja de tamal*, a corn husk, and tossed it in the *brasas*, the hot coal.

And I will never forget these mornings when I was a little boy and would wake up, sleepily walking into the kitchen, where she had this *jarrito*, this ceramic jar with chocolate, just cacao, water, and spices, standing in the glowing charcoal. My grandmother would ask, "You want some chocolate?" and I'd reply "Yes, please," and I could see the foam in the jar and smell that rich and delicious scent—that was home.

ARMANDO

I'm from a little town called Acatlán in the south of Puebla, Mexico. I have two sisters and one brother, I'm the youngest. My dad used to work for the government; my mom was a cooking teacher.

In my hometown there were always many people who went to the United States, and when they came back, they wore good clothes, bought cars, and built big houses. I was seventeen when I decided to leave too. Of course, my mother didn't want to let me go. She cried and asked, "Is it because we don't have much money?" but it wasn't that. I loved my life in my hometown—I just didn't see much of a future. We didn't leave because of the cartels and the crime. In my time that was all in the north of the country—now it's everywhere. We left because we were looking for opportunities.

I wasn't scared of crossing the border; I was hungry for new experiences and couldn't wait to go. It was a two-day bus ride from my town to the border, straight to Tijuana. In Tijuana, we looked for these guys called coyotes and paid $750 per person to cross. Nowadays, they want $13,000, but in the early '90s things were much simpler. We paid the guy, he took us in a van, and we crossed the border, just like that—we went from Tijuana straight to LA. There he bought me a plane ticket to New York, where my brother was living at that time. And that was it—end of story.

So now I was in New York, seventeen years old, everything was new. I didn't speak English and only knew my brother and a couple of people from my town. The only thing on my mind was to find a job, make some money, and send it to my mother. At first, I worked in a factory, but only for a week. Then, I worked in construction, but again, only for a week because I didn't like it. Eventually, somebody called me to work in a restaurant, and that's where it all began.

It was a small French restaurant called Pourette on Columbus Avenue. I started as a dishwasher and did that for three weeks. Then one of the prep guys left, and I asked the chef if I could have his place. For a year I worked as a prep cook, but I wanted to be a line cook. To get the chance, I began staying after my shifts without pay to help at the sauté station, the fryer, and the salad station. I wanted to learn, and I did.

In the kitchen there were many guys from Malaysia and just two Mexicans, so it was a bit divided because the Mexicans didn't speak much English. But, of course, the Malaysians taught me—after all, they got a free helper! (*Laughs.*) After a year of prepping and learning, an opportunity opened at the sauté station, and I got the job. By then, the chef knew that I liked to cook; it just always felt natural to me. I can walk into any kitchen and know what to do. I think that's because of my mother. In my hometown, my mother used to have what we call a *fonda*—a small restaurant where she sold food to the teachers. In the morning, she worked as a cooking teacher, and in the afternoon, she cooked in her *fonda*. She would often let me make *frescos* and juices. I would whip the eggs in the morning and clean the chilies in the evening.

Anyway, after three years at Pourette, I moved to another restaurant on Columbus Avenue, a more American-style one called Mackinac where I also worked on the line with a lot of Malaysian guys. By then, I was on the grill already. It was a busy place, especially on the weekends. From there I went to Perretti's, a small Italian restaurant where I was one of the strong line cooks. I had worked in a French and an American restaurant, and now I got into Italian cooking and started to understand the differences in the cuisines, and the more I learned the stronger I felt. I also started reading books and magazines because back then the internet wasn't a thing yet, and I wanted to discover new recipes. So, every Wednesday I would buy the *New York Times*. (*Laughs.*)

Here's a funny story. One night at Perretti's it was especially busy, and one of the chefs got so frustrated in that very small kitchen that he quit. He just left! (*Laughs.*) So, I took over, finished the shift, and after that I got a phone call and the opportunity to be the chef. That changed everything. After Perretti's, I got promoted to work at the Metropolitan Café. After three years there, I went to the Grill Room in the World Financial Center, and now I'm one of the executive chefs of the restaurant Robert. On the way, I didn't just learn about cooking, I also had to understand finances. As a chef, you are in charge of the payroll, food costs, and schedules—quite some responsibilities beyond cooking some delicious dishes. (*Laughs*.)

Besides all this, I had my family. I started very young, when I was nineteen years old. I met my wife here in New York. She is from Mexico City, her name is Graciela, and when she had our first daughter, my life changed completely. That's when I realized that I couldn't be prep or line cook forever because I needed more money, and I wanted my family to be proud of me.

A year later my second daughter was born. By then I did my regular shift and after that I worked part-time in another restaurant as a line cook to make extra money. My wife didn't work then—she took care of the babies, and we needed a bigger apartment. I worked two jobs for ten years.

At some point I told Graciela, "We need to buy a house—we can't rent forever." And then, thank God, we found and bought it. It's in the Bronx, and I bought it shortly before my thirtieth birthday. All of this—our family here, our home, and where I am professionally, it's such an amazing thing! (*Laughs*.) But, of course, I missed a lot of time with my family to get here. That time is gone. And, of course, I miss my hometown and my family. That's the sad part. That's what I lost.

My mom was a great cook. I love her *adobo* and so many of her dishes. It's all so different from here—the freshness of the ingredients, the beans, and those moments when the family sits together and eats. My mother used to make the *adobo* with pork ribs, *chile ancho*, and *chile pasilla*, and then she would add cloves and lots of avocado leaves.

She also made a fantastic *pipian*. She made it with chicken and ground the pumpkin seeds with a small *molino*. And her *pozole* with pork! It was green because she made it with *hoja santa*—these big, aromatic leaves that are also used in *tamales* or to wrap fish.

And then the fruits in my town! Our climate is tropical, so in every season we have different fruits, like *pitahaya*, dragon fruit, mangoes, and these huge incredible sweet watermelons! That's something I miss. Even though one can buy every kind of fruit here, it's not the same.

Over my years in New York, a few things really left a mark, and September 11 is one of them. At that time, I was working at the Grill Room in the World Financial Center, right next to the World Trade Center. My usual start time was nine o'clock, so when the first plane crashed, I was on the train. When I reached the bottom of the Twin Towers, the police didn't allow us to go through the tunnel. But I already had people working in the restaurant, and I was calling them, but they didn't answer. There were already problems with the connection.

I tried to go around to get into the restaurant, but they didn't let me. Then the second airplane hit. I saw everything. I was just standing there, with all the other people, in front of the Twin Towers. We felt the heat of the explosion. Then we started running—everybody just ran. I made it to Fulton Street and got into the Red Grill restaurant near South Street Seaport and the Sequoia. I knew most of the people there and tried to call my wife. Somehow, I got through. She answered. I said, "Listen, I'm fine," but she didn't know anything at that time. She was confused because my mother had called her from Mexico seconds before to ask her if I was fine, and she'd said yes and didn't understand. And now she turned on the TV.

By then I had realized how bad everything was and tried to go back again. I was on my way when the first tower collapsed. We all just ran. Luckily, everybody had gotten out of the restaurant. When I saw the second plane hitting the tower, I was scared. There were already people on the ground, I think, from the first explosion. More fell from the buildings, I saw them—I saw them jumping. I was crying. After that, for a couple of months, I often got emotional. I would just see something, anything, and wanted to cry. That was a scary time. They put me to work at Ernie's restaurant within a week after it happened. The Grill Room was closed for a year, I think. And at that time, for a moment, I was thinking of going back to Mexico. But then I thought, no, we are stronger than them.

We also navigated through COVID and came out stronger. I was the chef at Clyde Frazier's during that time, and like everyone else we had to close due to the pandemic. After a few weeks of just sitting around, I turned to my wife and said, "Listen, we need to do something." So that's what we did, right in the backyard of our Bronx house. One day, we came out with *tacos dorados* and empanadas from Venezuela because I had rented the second floor of our house to people from Venezuela. Essentially, we started a restaurant. We named it El Patio 3089, and it's even on Instagram. (*Laughs.*)

At first, everything was just to-go. But after two days, I saw people coming out again and again, so I went to BJ's and bought a flat grill. I told my wife, "OK, tomorrow we start selling real tacos." I ran to the store and bought pork, beef, and chicken, and I made three types of tacos on my flat grill in my backyard. Of course, I did most of the prep in our apartment. We sold sodas, beers, and so on. The whole thing got so popular that we were open every day!

The city never bothered us. Once, even a lady came and wrote an article about how people survive during the pandemic. (*Laughs.*) On weekends, we had two hundred people in our backyard with chairs and tables and all—not all at once of course. People just wanted to get out of their apartments, sit around in some backyard, meet friends, and eat some good, simple food. We were open for a couple of months, until I went back to work.

ALONSO

My name is Alonso. When I was a kid, they called me Poncho. I'm from El Salvador, from a town called Ilobasco in the center of the country. I went to school until ninth grade and left when I was seventeen. I wanted to go to college, but you needed money for books and other things, and my parents were poor. I'd worked in a small hardware store since I was ten years old. I used to work from eight in the morning till noon, then I went to school until six in the evening, and for these five hours of work in the store, I would get something between one and two dollars a day.

My life in El Salvador was generally okay, but back then, around twenty years ago, it was dangerous because of the gangs. Our *barrio* was divided between the MS-13 or Mara Salvatrucha, and LA-18. Our house was in the part of the MS-13, and my school was in the LA-18 part. On my way to school, they would often stop me. "What are you doing here?" "I'm just going to school." "But you live over there." Then they would beat me. If I was lucky, they would ask for money [instead of beating me]. The price to pass was ten *colon*, like one dollar. Sometimes I didn't go to school because I didn't want to give them money, and I didn't want to get beaten up either, and I couldn't do anything because they were five or six guys, you know. Every day, every day . . .

One time, two guys hit me hard—bam bam—and they took the Casio watch my sister Rosie had sent me from New York and my bike. It was a small used bike; I'd worked for it for a year. They took it, and there was nothing I could do. That's why I left, because of these things. It would have been easy to join a gang. They control everything, and they

31

get everything. You want girls? You want drugs or anything? They give it to you if you are one of them. But you have to do what they tell you.

I never even thought about going to the USA. Back then, the whole trip cost $6,000, and you had to pay half of it there and the other half after you got here, *if* you got here. So I never thought about it until one day. I worked together with my friend in the hardware store; it was a Sunday, early 2002. We'd worked together for a long time, and that day he told me: "Alonso, this will be my last day. I'll go to the USA." I couldn't believe it and asked him about it—how much was it? how did it work?—he explained. He was leaving on Friday. So I was thinking and thinking, and finally asked if I could come with him. He said, "That would be great, but let me talk to the guy, I will let you know tomorrow."

The next day he said, "OK, but you need the money." I didn't have the money, but now I really wanted to leave, so I called my sister in New York. Rosie said she could get the money next week, but the coyote wanted it on Wednesday, two days before leaving. Luckily, I had been saving. I had been working in the hardware store for seven years, and I hadn't given all the money to the gang members, and when my mom had asked me for money, I'd often said that I didn't have any, so I had $1,300 saved. I somehow convinced the coyote to take me with him for $1,500, and that I would pay the rest after I got here. My friend [lent] me the missing $200, and that was that.

I'd had a girlfriend over there for five years. I didn't say anything to her until Thursday, the very last day. I told her, "Tomorrow I will go to Estados Unidos. Today is our last day." She was very angry. "Why didn't you tell me before?" But I couldn't. It all happened so fast, and I had barely made it work with the money.

I left because life was just too difficult. I couldn't go to college and therefore wouldn't have found a good job, and then there were all these other problems. You couldn't even go to the park to relax because of these guys, the gangs. You only had a chance to live OK and without problems if you were part of a gang. And in those years, the police didn't do anything. These guys could rob you in front of them—they didn't care. When you went to the police station to say something, they didn't even listen. There was no life, no future. That's why I came here in 2002.

They picked us up Friday morning and drove us in a minivan to the border of Guatemala—my friend, me, and three other guys. We crossed with just our passports. In Guatemala, the coyote drove us near the border to Mexico to a house where more people were waiting. We stayed there for two days. They gave us food and brought more people until they said it's time to go, and we crossed into Mexico. We walked by night and crossed a big river.

In Mexico, we stayed in another house for two days, in a little town near the Guatemalan border. From there, they moved us to a big bus station—my friend, me, and the three other guys. They gave each of us a yogurt. You know, those yogurts in little plastic bottles? "Don't lose it," they said. "This is your yogurt. Always keep it in your hand when you are inside the bus."

We drove from the south of Mexico up to Puebla, and that was a long trip. I think it took us two days, and there were several checkpoints on the way. We were stopped three times, and it was very scary, but each time the same thing happened. They would stop the bus, go inside, and ask people for their IDs, but when they saw the yogurt in my hand, they just walked on. Same with my friends. Each time, the same thing. They saw the yogurt and said nothing. They were paid. The yogurt was a sign! (*Laughs.*)

In Puebla, we waited in a house for five days, and then we went to Mexico City, where we waited another three days in another house until they told us not to eat and drink because we would be brought to Agua Prieta—that's the border—in a truck, and they didn't want to stop on the way. It was one of these big trucks with a long trailer, and we hid in the tiny cabin behind the two drivers—my friend, me, and the three other guys. It was a very long drive, one day and one night, two thousand kilometers, and they only stopped for gas and once they bought some food for us. Then, we were finally there. It had taken me fourteen days from my hometown to the US border.

When we crossed, it got harder. The first time, we were a group of forty people. We started in the dark and walked through the desert for seven, eight hours. The next day, in the morning, Immigration saw us. The coyote had told us that if something like this happened, we should run away, anywhere, and if we could, we should follow him. So we ran and followed him, my friend and me and some other guys, about ten people. The coyote went back to Mexico so Immigration wouldn't get him. They caught a lot of people that morning, but not us, and not the coyote. And there we were, back in Mexico, in the same house.

Six days later, we tried again, but the guy, the coyote, didn't know what he was doing. Because we walked and walked, and then he didn't know where we were and where to go and called his friend, but his phone didn't work. He was lost. There was a little mountain, and he told us to go up there with him, but his phone didn't work there either. Finally, he said, "OK, guys, wait for me here. I will go back to my friend, and we will return together. You just wait here."

That was Tuesday, and there we were—my friend, me, and five other guys—on top of that mountain, seeing Immigration driving through the desert in the distance, and we waited. We had only water and no idea when and if the guy would come back.

Wednesday evening we ran out of water, so my friend and I went down the mountain to look for some, and we were lucky, miraculously lucky, because we found a tiny creek. Really tiny, but it had water. But then Thursday passed, and by Friday evening, we hadn't eaten for almost four days. So, all seven of us decided to go down to the street in the distance and let Immigration take us.

As we went down, desperate and starving, we saw the guy, the coyote—it was like a mirage, but there he was, with his friend, saying "Sorry, sorry" over and over again! And he brought food. He said he knew now where to go. (*Laughs.*) That night, we walked on for six hours or more until we saw city lights in the distance and waited nearby a highway. The coyote said, "You see, there is the United States already. That's Arizona."

In the morning, we got picked up by two cars. They brought us to a house. The drive only took thirty minutes, and there were showers and food. Two days later, we were moving again. They asked me where I wanted to go. I said Los Angeles because one of my cousins lived there, and Rosie by then had sent the rest of the first payment for the coyote to him.

And there I was, in Los Angeles. And what did I do? I started working. My cousin's father-in-law was making metal sinks and working spaces for restaurant kitchens, so the day after I arrived, I started helping him. I had learned welding in El Salvador from my grandfather, who made scissors, shovels, and things like that—all handmade. Now, I made $3,000 a month with that skill and could save $2,000 because I lived with my cousin's family and didn't have to pay rent. I felt good over there; I could have stayed. I worked Monday to Friday, and on Saturdays and Sundays we went to the park or the beach.

It was one Saturday morning, eight months after I got there. We were just preparing to go to the beach again when a friend of my cousin told him that he would go to New York the next day to deliver watermelons. So, I went from Los Angeles to New York in a truck full of watermelons. (*Laughs.*)

I came to New York in November 2002. I had really liked my life in LA, but most of my family was in New York. My sister Rosie lived in Queens. The first year was hard. I would often wake up thinking I was still in El Salvador or back again. It took me some time to fully adjust. I worked in a warehouse. In my twenty years in New York, I had only two jobs. My restaurant job is the second. The first one was the warehouse in Brooklyn. They sold clothes that came in big containers from China and India, and my job was to separate them by colors and sizes, put them in boxes, then place the boxes on pallets, and operate the forklift. They sold these clothes very cheap to Family Dollar, Sears, and Walmart. My life was apartment, working, apartment, working. It wasn't the best, but I didn't think too much about it because I knew so many people didn't make it. They couldn't leave, or they got sent back, or died on the way. I was lucky.

My sister's son is seventeen now, the same age I was when I left and came to the USA. But back then, I had a different mindset. When I was fifteen, oh my God, I had a mind like an adult. Compared to that, my sister's son is like a baby. (*Laughs.*) I think it's because his parents always protect him in everything. But when you have to survive as a nine-year-old in the streets of El Salvador, well, you learn a lot of things. It's a different life altogether. And of course, my parents were different too. They never said "I love you" or anything like this. They used to hit us, so . . . I had to take care of myself.

When I told my mother back then that I would go to the United States, she just said, "I can't say no, I can't say yes, because I don't give you money, you know how to go, God bless you." (*Laughs.*) On the last day, when I was leaving and got inside the minivan with the coyote, I don't know how, but my daddy cried and kept saying things like "I won't see you again" and so on. Even my mom cried. It was the first time they gave me a hug. But I didn't feel anything. I don't know why. It was as if I were going to the park and coming back later. I felt nothing.

Here, the mothers and fathers protect their kids too much, so by the time they're seventeen or eighteen, they still act like babies. "Mommy, when is dinner ready?" Mommy here, Mommy there . . . I experienced the other extreme. You know when I got my first pair of shoes? I was eight because I started school when I was eight years old. That's why I finished my ninth grade at seventeen. I started wearing shoes when I began going to school. Before that, I never wore shoes because nobody bought them for me. But here, my son, he has many, many shoes! (*Laughs.*) Of course, I wanted shoes before I turned eight. Some of my friends had shoes, and it felt strange to go into stores without wearing any. I even played soccer without shoes. But nobody got me any; I had to go to school first. (*Laughs.*)

I worked in that warehouse for sixteen years and started at Cookshop while I was still working there. Rosie told me about Cookshop in 2007, that they always needed bussers. But back then, my English was *no bueno*, and you need to speak a little English to interact with the guests, ask them if they need anything or if you can clean their table. So, from 2008 onwards, I had two jobs: Monday to Friday I worked from nine to four in the warehouse, and from Tuesday to Sunday I also worked from five to closing at Cookshop. On Saturdays, I worked the entire day at Cookshop. I quit the warehouse a couple of years ago, but I still have two jobs. Now, I work in my brother-in-law's cell-phone repair store. I never have a day off. The only time I didn't work for a few weeks was during the pandemic; that was the only break I had in twenty years. I came to New York to work, work, work . . .

I never want to go back to El Salvador. My mom and dad are here now too, and I have a wife and a son. Did you know that my wife is Chinese? And my boy is Chinese too! (*Laughs*.) I've known her since 2014. We met in the warehouse where she was helping out. I don't speak a lot of English; my wife speaks English okay, but she understands me. Our son speaks Chinese because his mother speaks Chinese with him. He speaks English because he goes to school, but he only speaks a *poquito* of Spanish. I don't want to talk in English with him because I want him to learn Spanish, and sometimes he runs to his mother saying: "Mommy, Daddy is not talking your language and doesn't want to talk my language!" He is five years old. I try to have more time for my family.

I have a house in my country. When I came here, I thought I would stay for maybe three to five years and then go back. So, at some point, I bought a house over there, paid it off, a little place in the city. But I don't think I will go back because I don't know anyone there anymore. There were five guys I went to school with, and we used to play chess together. Four of them are dead, killed by gangs or the cops, and the other guy went to North Carolina. All the young ones like me from that time either came here, or they died. So, if I go over there, there won't be anybody I know.

LUCIA

I was born in Atlixco, Puebla, which is two hours away from Mexico City. I came here with my mom when I was eleven years old. My dad was already living here. I am thirty-eight years old, and I have so many memories of Atlixco, especially of my grandmother and her cooking. One of the reasons I started working here at Rosie's is that it reminds me of my grandmother. She would get up at five every morning to make the tortillas, and I loved her *memelas*! When my grandmother called us to eat, everyone gathered around the table, the whole family. She was my mother's mother and had ten children, so it was a big family, and whoever was around would sit down for breakfast, lunch, or dinner. They all loved my grandmother's cooking.

I grew up with a lot of cousins, mostly boys, so I was a bit of a tomboy. (*Laughs.*) We had a real childhood; there were no iPads. We grew up climbing trees, playing in the dirt, and every time I came home from school, my mother made me *enfrijoladas*. That was my favorite snack. It's practically the grilled cheese sandwich for kids in Mexico. (*Laughs.*) It's just tortillas dipped in bean sauce with a topping like *queso fresco* or *crema fresca*. Very simple, but oh so good.

My father left when I was two years old, so I basically grew up without him. I was never really told why he left. My mom just used to say, "Your dad is away because he's trying to give you the best. He's working over there so we can have the things we didn't have." As a young child, you don't really understand that. You don't understand why your dad is away; you just miss him. You miss the love of a father. You wonder, "Where's my dad? I want to be with my dad."

Also, it wasn't easy for my mom to raise a kid by herself. She was sewing clothes on the side with one of those old sewing machines that you have to pedal. We were okay financially, but she needed a partner. And I needed a father, a father figure that I could be with physically and hug, not only talk to on the phone once in a while.

So, one day, when I was eleven years old, my mom said, "Hey, what do you think? Your dad is over there, and we haven't seen him in so long. Should we move to New York to be with him?" I just said, "*Si! Si!* I want to be with my dad!"

We came like everyone else, illegally. I'm not going to lie. We crossed the border in Arizona. Honestly, it wasn't that hard back then. My mom always tells me, "You thought we were just traveling. You had no worries. You were just a kid." For me, it was an adventure. It was all so exciting because the grown-ups would constantly say, "Don't do this. Don't be suspicious. Let's hide." (*Laughs.*)

In New York, I met my father, which was very emotional. It was like two different emotions at the same time. I was very happy to be with him again, but at the same time, he was a stranger to me. He was a man I hadn't seen in years, even though we had spoken almost every day on the phone. It was like, "Who is this man?" It took me a while to connect with him, and it's just as you grow older that you understand the sacrifices your parents made to give you the best they could, even though it sometimes means not having the love of a father.

In New York, everything was new to me: a new country, new language, new school, new people. In Mexico, I had been very good in school. There, they picked the best students to carry the flag every Monday in the schoolyard while the anthem was being sung, and I carried the flag many times. Now, I didn't even know the language. Everything was just very intimidating. I don't know if you can be depressed as a kid, but I think I was a little depressed. I just wanted to go back to Mexico.

My father was very strict, and when he put me in an English-only class because he thought I would learn faster that way, it just made it all worse for me. After a while, my mom decided that I should change to a bilingual class. Luckily, New York is very diverse, so in school, you would find different kids from different countries, including kids whose parents were from Mexico. Also, we lived in Astoria, which is a mixed neighborhood with a lot of Greeks, Italians, and Spanish-speaking people. This helped me a lot, and things got better.

My dad has always been a very hardworking man. He worked as a dishwasher, busser, and food runner, and he did everything with dignity. He would always say, "You have to take pride in what you do, even if you're just a dishwasher, because you're making a living." He would come home and say, "Today was a very busy day, but you know what? I got the job done." This approach to work is one of the things I learned from him.

I started working in the restaurant business when I was seventeen years old and still in high school. I began as a coat check in one of David Bouley's restaurants in downtown Manhattan, an Austrian restaurant called Danube, because one of my half brothers was working there. I worked as a coat check for three years, and then Bouley opened another restaurant called Bouley Upstairs. I applied for a job there, started working as a busser, and after a while, I got promoted to food runner and expediter. At this point, I was twenty-two years old and went to school to become a medical assistant.

I never did become a medical assistant, though. I graduated, did an internship for three months, and liked it, but I also realized that it wasn't for me. I wanted to keep working in restaurants. I think what attracts me to the restaurant business and keeps me interested is that it gets me out of my comfort zone. I've always been an introverted, quiet person, with maybe even a little bit of social anxiety, and my work in restaurants has always forced me to meet new people and introduce myself to them.

At Bouley Upstairs, I eventually started working as a server and did that for five years. It was fascinating because it was a small restaurant with maybe twenty-five seats and an open kitchen where Chef Bouley was cooking, kind of doing his show, and the food was really good—very simple, but people loved it. We used to get a lot of famous guests there.

I left Bouley because they closed the restaurant. My next job I found the old-fashioned way, on Craigslist. (*Laughs.*) It was a place called Danji in Hell's Kitchen, the first Korean restaurant to ever get a Michelin star in New York. It was small too—I always liked small restaurants. I worked there for eight years, then the pandemic happened. In a way, it was the best thing for me because it made me see that I needed a change in my life. I realized that if I wanted to keep working at restaurants, I needed to be more than a server.

I left Danji and started working as a server at Le District by the World Trade Center. After one year, when one of the managers was leaving, I asked the general manager to give me the opportunity to become a manager. He took a chance on me, saying, "You've never been a manager before, but everybody starts from somewhere." So, I started working as a manager, and a month later, I was promoted to assistant general manager.

Sometimes I think about how far I've come—from the little girl who came home from school in Mexico happy to eat her *enfrijoladas* to being a manager under a famous chef in New York. I have to say, I'm proud of myself. I basically started from the bottom, and here I am. I think it was a combination of good luck and hard work. Things happen because, yes, luck exists, but also hard work always shows, and people see it.

People always ask me, "What's your favorite Mexican restaurant?" And I'm like, "I don't have one." Because, for a Mexican, the best Mexican restaurant is at home. (*Laughs.*) Like my mother's *enchiladas suizas*—they are just the best. And oh, her *pozole blanco*! She used to cook it only once or twice a year; that's how complex it is to make.

Now I have to go to Mexico to eat her food. My parents moved there two months ago. Yes, they went back. My dad is seventy-three years old, and I told him, "Listen, you have worked your whole life. I think it's time for you to stop and start enjoying life." They have their house there, and—well, that conversation was very emotional, and so was their leaving. When they left, my mom said, "I can't believe I brought you here as a little kid, and now I'm leaving without you."

I'm not sure if I would move back to Mexico at some point. Maybe I'm too much of a New Yorker by now. My dream is to open my own place, maybe a coffee shop with lots of plants. My mom always had many plants; they were hanging everywhere. She watered them every morning. So, I love plants, and I would love to have my own place, something I have worked hard for and that is truly mine, even if it's just a small café.

I only returned to Mexico once, five years ago, for a short visit to Atlixco. It was very different. The city had changed, and the school looked old. It's not as safe as it used to be. There are kidnappings and cartels. Of course, it worries me that my parents are there now, because you never know who's watching or who is around. I tell them not to go out much and to try to be safe. But it is what it is. You have to live with it and try not to live in fear. And people are trying their best. That's the best part of everything. Always, no matter what, people are always trying to do their best.

Now I have a good reason to visit Mexico more often. And I will not only see my parents; I also want to explore the country. I would love to go to Oaxaca. I don't know why. (*Laughs.*) Everybody's always talking about Oaxaca, especially about the food there. I wouldn't go to a fancy restaurant, though; I would try to eat in somebody's house because that's where you get the best food. Often, the simple is better.

LIGORIO

My name is Ligorio. I am from a small town near the city of Cuenca, Ecuador. The name of my town, from an Inca word, is Chiquintad. The conquistadors named the city Cuenca after the Spanish city with the same name. From what I understand, as the popular story goes, the area resembled their homeland because of the rivers and mountains in this part of Ecuador. Cuenca is inland, about three or four hours' driving time from the coast. My early memories of family life were almost entirely of farming and being in the cornfields. My father always had horses, cows, and sheep along with the many chickens that my mother raised—and of course we had the famous Ecuadorian guinea pig, the *cuy*. The cuy is a traditional food from the Andes, so it was just another food source available to us. I always had things to do to help either in the house or in the fields. As a child, I collected wood for my mother to cook with. Of course, we didn't have gas—cooking was always done with wood. My grandparents, aunts, and uncles—the entire extended family—used wood to cook with. This is something I remember distinctly.

I have two older sisters and one younger sister. I don't remember things as being particularly difficult. My father never had a regular job—our family was dependent on what could be sold from the farm, the things that we raised or cultivated. But I remember being happy, going to the mountains or the nearby rivers—there were neighbors and relatives [and] that allowed us to create games and have fun playing together. So, I remember those times where work was very important: children were relied on to help in the house, in the fields, and with the care for the animals. But we also had time to play. We always had food on the table and a roof over our heads, but I knew it was necessary to help.

There was a period in the area I'm from where people simply did not believe in sending their children to school. Especially in my father's time, education was not valued. It was important for people to have large families because there was no other way to get their farmwork done. There was no other way to accomplish the necessary farmwork—there was no such thing as hiring farmhands. If the work wasn't achieved there was no food and no income. My relationship with my parents was good, especially with my mother. I was never able to consider my father as a friend or someone to confide in. The relationship was always about work—what he wanted done and how things should be done, of course his way only! (*Laughs.*)

Eventually, the idea of sending children to school became more acceptable. The city began to provide more teachers, so gradually more kids from my town started going to school. Going to school didn't stop the need for farmwork though—we had to get up in the morning around 4:30 to start feeding the animals. I remember collecting fresh grass for the little piglets. The time spent in the early morning taking care of the animals was a form of homework for me. Once finished, we were able to go off to school. I liked school very much. I was able to get away from the labor that was still very much a part of my life. Then, of course, when we returned from school we had to go to the fields and collect the animals and bring them back to the house. Agriculture was our means of survival, as well as for all the other people in my small town. Maize, wheat, potatoes, and beans—those were the primary things we grew and the things that to this day people are dependent on.

I assumed from an early age that my life was going to be about farming, working in the fields, taking care of the animals, [and] growing produce for the market, as my father and grandparents had done. To this day, I can say that I didn't judge my life. I loved working in the fields—my life was good. When I return to Ecuador to visit, the thing that brings back the most meaningful memories is the chicken soup that my mother makes. Returning to Ecuador every two years or so remains important for me, as settled in New York as I am—it's where I'm from, and my wife is from Uruguay, so the connection is important.

But things began to change for me when I started high school. I always liked machines as a young child. There was a subject called Precision Machines where I learned how to use a lathe, various types of drill presses, and welding—I loved it. Not to brag, but I was always the first to complete the assigned tasks that were given. Making things that had to have precise measurements was something that fascinated me. There was an important connection to this type of skill that happened almost immediately. I believed with the skills I learned in high school there was so much that I could do. Those skills that I learned in high school led to the first job I had as a young adult. I worked for a company in the neighborhood as a welder that built door frames, stairs, and gates—many people had gates for security. I still had to help my father in the field, but now I was getting paid for my work welding [while also] working in the fields and finishing high school. At that time, there were constant conversations among many of the young people that I knew to go to the US. There was a boom among young people to go to the US. I had a good life in Ecuador, but I was curious to know about other places, so I went to Venezuela instead after high school and worked in Caracas for five years. That is when my life started—well, let's say the "fun life." (*Laughs.*) Living under the eye of my father, I never went out—he was so strict and controlled every part of my life. In fact, one time, I went to a party without telling my father and he caught me at four in the morning trying to sneak back into the house. That was the first and last time that happened—my father was so strict.

When I went to Venezuela, I finally felt free—but I knew the difference between right and wrong. Caracas was incredibly beautiful at the time. My sister worked for a wealthy family, and I got a job taking care of the property, the gardens, the pool—whatever was necessary. Then I started doing side jobs—welding, building staircases, the type of work that I was doing in Ecuador. For almost the first year and a half, I almost never went out in public. I went out once before I became a legal resident and had to run out of the back door of a city bus as four policemen entered. The immigration laws were so restrictive.

For example, the police would ask for documents of people riding the buses—you could be deported almost immediately if you weren't in the country legally. Life was good at that time in Venezuela: salaries were three to four times that of Ecuador, [and so] many Ecuadorians went to Venezuela. This was before Hugo Chávez. The president at the time I was there was Carlos Andrés Pérez. At that time Venezuela was booming. Chávez began the ruin of the country.

My father remained a central figure in my life even when I was living in Venezuela. As an example, he came to Caracas unannounced on a day that I had plans with many friends to go to the beach—this was an important day for me, especially since I didn't have to work. My sister called and told me I had to come home: "Papa is here!" I was twenty-three or twenty-four at the time, and he was still trying to control my life. As he said when I reluctantly saw him, "I came to Venezuela because I was concerned you were ruining your life." Even at that age, he was trying to control me. That day, though, it was necessary to confront him and tell him as a grown man [that] he had to step back from trying to control my life. In fact, I remember asking him if he thought he was some sort of perfect person—the perfect teenager, the perfect father? And I knew I had to free myself from the fear of him beating me or, more importantly, continuing to direct my life. This was an important turning point for both of us, especially when he traveled all the way to Venezuela unannounced to intrude on me and the decisions I was making for myself. It was difficult, but I think he finally understood how important it was to let go. (*Laughs.*)

The following year, after almost five years of living and working in Venezuela, I decided to go to the US. Traveling to the US was always something I had in my mind to do eventually—I wanted more. The salaries in Ecuador were always so low. Venezuela was better but listening to people talking about the opportunities available in the US—I heard repeated conversations about the wages that were available from working in restaurants. Even though the thought of going to the US remained in my mind, I was basically content with my life in Caracas.

One day my cousin, who had worked in the US, came to me after his return from New York and said, "Let's go—I'm going to go back to the States next week." I thought for a moment and agreed almost on the spot. Within the week we were in Guatemala, where we spent almost a month waiting to hear about traveling preparations with a coyote. We traveled by bus through Mexico to Matamoros, where I stayed for about two weeks. Then I swam across the Rio Bravo* to Brownsville, Texas. I was so concerned about being caught by the Immigration agents, but everything went smoothly, and the coyote arranged tickets for me to fly to New York. It was relatively easy at that time once in the States—I don't even recall being asked for identification for the flight to New York.

My goal was to find a restaurant job in New York City. At first, I couldn't find anything—at that time, it was not easy to find work. I finally found a job shining shoes in Times Square. I had never shined shoes in my life, but it was the only thing I could find—being paid $1.50 per hour, working about twelve hours a day. Speaking no English, I was making $200 to $300 a day in tips. One weekend after work I went to play soccer with some friends. I couldn't walk the next day, after having done nothing athletic for months—my body ached, I was so sore I was unable to get out of bed for almost two days. I didn't show up for my shoeshine job and had no way of contacting my boss and of course I spoke no English. I was fired when I finally went back—the owner told me to go play soccer since that was more important. From working with precision machines to shining shoes.

From there I went to work at a Korean restaurant on the West Side of Manhattan, washing dishes and making deliveries—remember, I spoke no English, just the basics: "hello," "good morning," "how are you?" I was constantly getting lost while making deliveries—no bicycle, walking in the snow, completely unfamiliar with the neighborhood, the house numbers, not being able to find the customer, going back to the restaurant and getting yelled at by the owner. When there were no deliveries, I helped in the kitchen, chopping onions or broccoli. I worked about eleven hours a day. Then I got another job as a dishwasher at an Italian restaurant called Pasta Presto, also owned by Koreans. The owner really pushed me, cleaning the kitchen, mopping floors, windows . . . it

---

* Rio Grande River

was hard work, but I didn't care. I was young and I was making three dollars an hour.

Then I found a job in a factory, sewing buttons and zippers onto clothing. I never had used a sewing machine before, but I watched and learned by seeing how the other people used the machines. I practiced one day and the next I was sewing along with the other workers. I started making $3.50 an hour. Then, because of my skill, I made $4.00 an hour. I worked at Pasta Presto at night and the factory during the day—on the weekends I went to school for English. My hands were busy. (*Laughs*.) Sometime later, I left the factory and stayed at Pasta Presto for about five years because my wage increased to $4.50 an hour and I was able to go to school for English full-time. I stayed there that amount of time because the schedule was flexible—it allowed me to go to school and make enough money to live on at the time. One day I had a strong verbal fight with a manager. It was probably interesting to hear me arguing using my broken English, but I decided to leave.

Then I started working as a busboy in an Italian restaurant where I also made tips along with my hourly wage. I liked working in restaurants, but I knew deep down that it wasn't the direction that I wanted to continue to take for my life. While working as a busboy, I started to go to refrigeration school—I sensed that there was a future in having that skill and I knew I had a talent for all types of machines. I went back to the owner of Pasta Presto, who had five restaurants, and offered to start working on the refrigeration in his restaurants. About that time was when I started working for ARK Restaurants.* I met Vinny Pascal (one of the owners of ARK Restaurants) at a restaurant called Jim McMullen's. I walked in and noticed a guy standing at the bar and told him I was looking for a busboy or waiter job. I didn't know for some time that he was one of the owners of the restaurant group. He sent me down to South Street Seaport where ARK had just opened a new restaurant called Sequoia. "Go down to Sequoia and tell them that Vinny sent you." My English was good, and I started making great

---

* ARK Restaurants is a large group that operates restaurants in a number of different states, including New York.

money at Sequoia—a very busy place. At some point later, I mentioned to Vinny that I had gone to school for refrigeration. Little by little I began to do maintenance for the group. One thing led to another. God gave me these abilities and I just continued to work at it. I'm able to do plumbing, welding, electrical, refrigeration, woodworking—I wanted to always continue learning and not get stuck on one thing, but I always liked what I was doing. Everything was an opportunity, and, really, refrigeration led to so many things because it requires an understanding of many different technical skills.

My satisfaction is knowing that my customers are happy. It has been a privilege working for ARK. Vinny is like my godfather—he believed in me, and it has been a privilege knowing Chris [Paraskevaides], Vicki [Freeman], and you [Marc Meyer].

DIANA

My name is Diana and I'm from Bucaramanga, Colombia. It's a beautiful city in the north-central part of the country with many parks, and one of the parks, the Parque del Agua, has a waterfall and many fountains. I lived almost my entire life in Bucaramanga. One of the things that my city is known for is the handmade jewelry that is produced there and the design and production of shoes and handbags by skilled leather workers. Also, there is an incredibly stunning natural wonder of the country called Chicamocha. It is a steep canyon with a river that runs through the bottom of the canyon. It attracts artists from all over the country because of the natural beauty of the area—and sports like river rafting and bungee jumping are popular there. Chicamocha is considered a national treasure.

I loved going to school, I loved to study, I was a good student, but I was a crazy, wild child—it was impossible for me to stop moving. Definitely a tomboy, playing soccer, running, climbing trees, picking up mangoes that had fallen. My friends and I played in the nearby mountains, imagining ourselves as different characters and making up stories that we were adventurers discovering places, plants, and animals that no one had known of before—I felt incredibly free at that time. I would return home with my legs covered with small thorns and grass spurs from playing in the new lands that we had found in our childhood world. My memories of childhood are good.

I became pregnant with twins at the age of fifteen, and I decided to go to school anyway. I was in the tenth grade, and I wanted to go to school pregnant—I didn't care. People said, "Oh my God, you're pregnant and you're only fifteen," but I wanted to have those two girls. My parents were not happy because I had won a scholarship to go to Switzerland for the eleventh grade, which I had to give up. My mother wanted me to have an abortion—she didn't want me to go through with the pregnancy. Abortion was not legal in Colombia at that time, but my mother didn't care. She made it clear that I had failed her. At that moment, it was confirmed by ultrasound that I was going to have twins. My father still did not know that I was pregnant—my mother believed it was important to keep this information from him because he had a weak heart. I remember crying and crying at the gynecologist's office—I went to the bathroom to be alone, away from my mother, and I prayed. . . . I wanted these babies, and I was not going to have an abortion. I knew I wanted to be a mom. When everything was confirmed my mother's response was, "You have to get married."

We arrived home from the doctor. My father was not there—at that time he was traveling. His work was, and still is, in pharmaceutical sales to doctors' offices. My mother called my boyfriend: "Luis, Diana is pregnant, and you will have to marry her. I'll wait here to discuss this with you." I didn't want anything more to do with him—he was eighteen and I was fifteen. He was an adult by Colombian law, but I was a child. Even though he acted like a child, he accepted his responsibility and agreed to marry me, saying, "I love her, and I want to be a father." It would have been very easy for him to deny being the father at that time. I remember that I didn't like Luis, but at least he acted like an adult.

I know I disappointed my parents. My mother cried a lot, but she didn't cry for me—she was more worried about how this would affect my dad. She didn't care about me. You know I had many dreams and hopes for my life, but in that moment, I felt completely alone, particularly because my mother was unable to show any love. She showed no sympathy; she couldn't give love. She loved my dad—but I was this fifteen-year-old girl facing huge responsibilities without the support of my mother. Through all my experiences I've learned how to give love, especially to my daughters.

The ability to look back and see more clearly has taken me many years. I know that my mother did not give me the love that I needed.

My mother was very physically aggressive towards me. She hit me as if I was a boy—I know this is the way she was treated as a child. This is not the life I wanted for myself or my daughters. These experiences helped to create a commitment within me to raise my daughters with love, a promise to give what I didn't get—what I didn't in that moment have.

The next man I was with, despite his religious beliefs, was also abusive. Religion couldn't save this man from the way he treated me. It was clear to me at this point [that] I didn't need a man to succeed in life—but so many people around me said I would not get another man because I had three daughters. I was warned, "No one will want a woman with children." So, I began—I went to school at night and worked during the day. I did so many things—I sold cell phone minutes in front of the university while I was pregnant with my third daughter; I sold ice cream; I sold pajamas. After that I sold magazine subscriptions in a mall—that was considered a very professional job. Then I was selling clothes and accessories for professional women—that's when my personal goal began to take shape. I wanted to go to university and become a professional person.

My life was about work and study. Fortunately, my mother began to help take care of my daughters. I believe I have a relationship with my mother because I realized I needed to show her the love that she never had. This was somehow a skill that I developed over time, but I taught myself. She never experienced love as a child, but as I loved my daughters—through my desire to be a good mother to my children—I was able to show my mother love as well. God gave me this opportunity, in a sense, to be, in a way, a loving parent to my mother. So, I have been able to find great love for my mother, along with the realization that more is to be accomplished with love than with hate. I had to free myself from the things that people said to me about being a pregnant child or the men that abused me [or] the poor relationship I had with my mother—if these things remained in my life, I knew I could not achieve my goals.

I gradually learned more about my mother's childhood. She was the oldest of ten children, basically becoming another parent for her younger brothers and sisters—dressing them, cooking and cleaning. I don't believe she had a real childhood. Then there was my father, a very handsome man—a "muscle guy," you know, a weight lifter. He represented Colombia in weight lifting. But he was a cheating guy. The social attitude then was to accept this type of behavior because a woman needed a man, regardless. I think many women in Colombia have very [few] choices outside of raising children. I insisted that that was not going to be my case. I was breaking the rules—it wasn't that I set out to break the system, I just knew that was not the life for me. I had to fight against the concept that there was no other identity for a woman other than to be a mother.

I raised three very strong, independent young women. My girls believe that they are contributing to Colombian society because of their intelligence, not because they are having babies—they prefer cats! (*Laughs.*) I didn't really see myself as a victim of society. There is a difference in my mind—I did suffer, though, in some way, but I was able to break from it. I'm not sure exactly how I found the mentality to escape this vision of Colombian women—I knew that I could do something else with my life. Also, I continued to see my father as a cheating guy, and I wasn't going to be a woman who accepted that type of relationship—I hated that. I would prefer to be alone than with someone who cheated on me—and women should not be silent in a society that accepts that behavior among men.

I am forty-one—I came to the US about two years ago. That is part of the adventuresome person that I am, that is perhaps the masculine nature in me, that is in all people. I had a successful career in Colombia, but I needed more. My nature is fire, energy, the masculine part I mentioned. With the success I was having as a professional, the company I was working for transferred me to Bogotá, the capital. Then, following the pandemic, to advance further professionally, it was necessary for me to come to the US to attend school for English.

I began in the US by cleaning high-fashion clothing boutiques, and in the evening, I worked in a restaurant restocking clean glassware. It was a shocking change for me from the life I had in Colombia. At first it was also difficult to see the lives that many Latin Americans and Mexicans were living—many sharing rooms to sleep, traveling on the subway long distances, working in hot kitchens, or overnight cleaning. But I had goals. I was running a race, and it was impossible to consider quitting. I had to take the next step—cleaning and restocking in a restaurant wasn't part of my goal. To make more money in the restaurant, I knew I had to eventually become a server—but I had to lose my fear that my English was not good enough. Being a host was the next step: that's where I could make many mistakes, but I could improve my ability to speak English. Losing my fear was one part of the challenge of living and working in New York. The other was that I had to accept that I could not rely on the identity I had as a professional, educated career woman in Colombia.

How could I break out of just being host or re-stocker? What must I do? So, I took the menus home and studied every word, to know and understand every ingredient. I impressed the manager so much with my effort and knowledge that I was given an opportunity the next day. That's my attitude. I will not give up—I will achieve my goals.

MAMADOU

I was born in Ivory Coast, but my parents are from Burkina Faso, and I
was raised between both countries. Compared to an American family,
my family is huge. My dad is a Muslim, and in that religion, it's not a
must, but if you want and have the means . . . Well, my dad has four
wives. My mum is the second, with three kids. All in all, my father's
kids, I think we are seventeen. In my society, we usually don't use words
like *half brother* or *half sister.*

I was a happy kid—we all were. My father had a transportation
business and owned farmland. We lived in a town a couple of kilometers away from Abidjan, the capital of Ivory Coast, and we lived better
than most. We never lacked food or clothing. We had clean water and
electricity, and we all went to school. It was a good life. Then, in 2010,
the Ivorian crisis began, turned into the Second Ivorian Civil War,
and everything changed. I was already in my early twenties when that
happened.

It was like during the lockdown here in America—everything
stopped. My father's business declined, and the life we were used to
wasn't available anymore. We were lucky—we didn't experience the
violence firsthand, but my dad took his economic downfall hard. He
was not the man he used to be. It was heartbreaking and painful to see
my family's decline and not be able to do something to help. At some
point, I just knew I had to leave to be able to support them. This is
where it all started.

I came to the United States with a student visa. My brother and
his wife already lived in New York, and they had told me about the

opportunities you can have here. They said that if you know where you are coming from, you will always be able to get somewhere. Plus, I felt close to American culture. In Africa, we watch American movies and love basketball. I idolized Michael Jordan, Kobe, and Carmelo Anthony, who used to play for the Knicks back then. And suddenly, I was here, in New York. My first impression was: "Wow." My second: "I made it." My third: "It's cold!" (*Laughs.*)

I had never experienced this kind of cold. I was wandering through the city for days, amazed at everything. Everything was so different, especially the people. Here is a fun fact: at the beginning, when I saw certain groups of people—like Asians or Latinos—they all looked alike to me. It took me some time until I was able to differentiate them. (*Laughs.*)

Emotionally, the beginning wasn't easy. I spent so much money calling my parents, I had to cut back until I only called them twice a month. Family means everything to me, as it does for most Africans. We were raised to stick together and be there for each other, but I was so homesick that I had to cut ties with my family to be able to focus on what I was here for.

My first job was in a Jamaican restaurant. I was happy to have one after walking through the city for weeks, asking people for work in vain, until I used an agency. I paid them, they got me my first job, but I didn't know what the job was about. (*Laughs.*) They said the word, but since I didn't speak English well, I didn't understand. So, I was just happy—until I came to work. At first, I was in shock, and then I started laughing. I was working as a dishwasher! I had to wash the dishes and clean the kitchen!

You know, where I come from, that's women's work. No man ever does that. We can't even cook. All that kind of work is done by our mothers or sisters. And here I was, remembering how my mom once asked me to help her clean, and I said no, and now I was scrubbing surfaces and washing dishes to make a living, realizing how hard that work was! (*Laughs.*)

I didn't think this work was below me, though. Instead, I remembered my father telling me, "No matter how dirty a job is, once you've done the job, once you get home, you take a shower, put on fresh clothes, and you are you again. You made your living—that's self-respect, that's honor."

I also had to learn how to cook for myself. Nobody was doing that for me anymore either! So, I called my sisters and my mom, asked girls I knew, and went to YouTube to learn. I only cook African dishes, like rice with okra sauce or peanut butter stew, or *babenda*, a traditional dish from Burkina Faso and one of my family's favorite foods. It is prepared using fermented locust beans like *dawa dawa* or tamarind, fish, and bitter greens like spinach or kale. From Ivory Coast, I love *acheke*, a traditional side dish made from fermented cassava pulp. When it is dried, it is a bit like couscous. You eat it with fish and chicken, or whatever you like. And then there is *placali*, a fermented cassava paste that I've never cooked, but my roommate does, and I will try it too. If I put my mind to it, I can do it.

[I've been] in the US for almost ten years now. I work as a server. I'm grateful for what I've accomplished, and when I walk into the kitchen, I value everybody in there, because I know how it is, what it takes. When I get to the dishwasher's station and have the time, I put the food waste in the trash can and stack the plates for him to ease his load.

I have family here: my brother, his wife, and their kids. I'm not alone. In my free time, I go to the gym, I cook, I watch TV, and sometimes I meet with friends. But I'm a rather private person; it's kind of hard for me to open up to people. During the winter, I don't really leave my apartment, only to go to work or the gym. I work out a lot; that has always helped me.

I am thirty-five years old now, and I am not married. I am still looking for the right woman. I want somebody with whom I can grow and who can grow around me, somebody who brings out the best in me and I bring out the best in her, who is God-fearing and loves family. I have met some girls who could have been the one, but some I knew too late; they were already married and had kids. Others were looking for financial security, and sometimes your revenue is not what they are seeking.

I'm here, I'm working, I help support my family—my mom and my dad. My next goal is to have my own structure, my own business. A friend of mine owns a couple of trucks and maybe we can put some money together and buy a new one. I also want to do business in Africa. I'm thinking about poultry farming; there is money in that. I'm doing everything in my power so I can succeed. I want my mom to be able to go outside and walk around happily, knowing that her son is doing well.

I miss so much about Africa: the life, the love, the food—pretty much everything. But it pains me to see my continent because it's doing badly. Africa is so blessed and rich, but our politicians ruin everything, and old contracts bleed us dry. We have so much potential. Only two African countries—Ghana and Ivory Coast—produce 70 percent of the world's cocoa. And Burkina Faso is one of the biggest producers of cotton and gold in the world. But agreements have been signed that allow France and other countries to take all the gold, cotton, and cocoa, leaving African countries with only a fraction of the revenue. We are being robbed. It's still a colonial relationship. When will it end?

I haven't been back since I left; I must sort out my documentation first. My father is old now. We are grateful that he is still around, even if he isn't doing anything right now. He doesn't have to. We support him.

There are many things I want to do in Africa. I want to build my business, poultry farming, to be independent and [be] able to help others, but I need money to buy the land and everything. I would like to do both—have a business here in the US and one back home, going back and forth. I trust my vision; I know I will do great. And maybe I can find somebody by telling my story here who wants to invest in me—*inshallah*.

JOSÉ

I was born in Mexico City. When I was three years old, my father crossed the border. A year later, my mom took me and my younger sister, and we followed him on the same route. My father left Mexico because he was in a gang in a top position, while my uncle, who would later play an important role in my life, was in a rival gang. And even though family always came first, there were issues. So, when my father's second child, my sister, was born, he and my uncle left to the United States together, to New York.

One of my earliest memories is my mother explaining to me that we had to leave our home. I recall the crossing; she carried my sister on one arm while holding me with her other hand, and we walked for long days. Then, I remember us staying in a hotel and eating pizza. To this day, my mom doesn't eat pizza because we had it for three days in a row—it was all they were giving us. (*Laughs.*)

In New York, we lived in a three-bedroom apartment in Queens with two other families, one family per bedroom. There were many rules, like not turning on the lights when it's not necessary, and we mostly ate beans and rice; things like meat or avocados we had only on Fridays or payday.

My mom was at home while my dad worked in a restaurant in Brooklyn off the D train, so it was a long commute—an hour and thirty minutes during the day, and an hour and forty-five minutes coming back. I remember the commute well because years later, I made it too. My father started as a dishwasher and worked his way up to become a chef.

As the man of the house, he had to provide for us. He didn't speak much; he kept to himself, but you could see that something was troubling him; he drank a lot. When I became aware of our situation, I started to ask questions. Why did I have to wear the same pair of sneakers the entire year while others had three? Why did other families own a car, and we didn't? Why could I only have two tortillas for dinner?

I quickly realized that it was a monetary problem. Trying to solve it, I researched in books, and soon I knew what Social Security was, a weekly paycheck, a minimum wage, and so on. Of course, I couldn't solve the problem, but I did my best to protect my sister. While my friends were playing, I was focused on surviving. When we were hungry, I would go to the pizza man and ask him, "Hey, man, can I get a slice? I will pay you on Saturday." I would tell my sister stories about why we didn't have more to eat, and a few times, I even went to a deli and stole some things, you know. I'm not proud of it, but we were hungry, and it needed to be done. It was us being hungry, needing toilet paper, shampoo, or soap.

I was always a good student, got good grades, and tried my best. But it's hard to pay attention when you're hungry. And that's a significant memory, being hungry. I learned English in school and from watching TV. As I got better, my Spanish was getting worse because, at the same time, I was speaking less and less with my parents. Back then, we barely spoke; there was no communication. What I felt was a mixture of hunger, anger, and distance. That's how I lost my Spanish. I gained it back years later when I worked in restaurants.

When I was in seventh grade, I got bullied a lot. I went to LAC High School (Martin Luther King Jr. High School), and there were three projects around the school—it wasn't easy. And bullying wasn't a thing like it is today. Teachers didn't do anything—people just turned their heads, and I was coming home with bruises and [was] generally miserable. One day, my father bought me a brand-new North Face jacket, and two days later, I came home without it—they had stolen it. That's when my father decided that I needed to work to become more manly. He basically dragged me into the restaurant where he worked. I was twelve years old, and that's how I started.

I started with weekends: Fridays after school and all day Saturday, for twelve to fourteen hours. At first, I was cleaning. My father would tell me to clean a wall, then he came and said, "I told you to clean the wall and not to massage it," and he yanked the towel out of my hand and showed me how to really get in there. Later, he let me cut onions and clean calamari.

My Sundays were about church and catching up on sleep. We were Catholic back then. Then my mother decided we would become Christian. That caused a noticeable change in my life, because after that, things got better. My mom started to be more positive. She started talking to my dad more. And before that, it was tough to get a hug or a kiss or any kind of affection from my parents, but the new religion softened them. My mom still goes to church four times a week.

While in my family things got slightly better, I took my anger and started lifting weights. I got really strong and started to fight back in school. I didn't become a bully, but I became known as someone who, if you pick a fight with him, he will fight back.

I worked in my father's restaurant until I was sixteen. In the summers I worked the whole week, sixty hours, and now I did more serious stuff, like prepping and cooking and working in the service, until I decided that I wanted to do something on my own.

After a failed attempt at a deli, where the manager immediately fired me because I had greeted my first customer, an older lady, with the words, "Hey, what do you want?" my uncle helped me get a job. I desperately needed one because I was about to start college and needed a computer and other things, and my sister needed support too. So, my uncle, the one who used to be in a gang in Mexico, took care of me. He was working in one of the restaurants at the Museum of Modern Art as a prep cook, and he got me a job as an overnight porter. I was seventeen by then.

One day this gentleman, who was part of the house, was walking by, stopped, looked at me and said, "Hey, you are not going to make it past twenty-five breathing these chemicals. Why don't you apply for something else?" I answered, "I don't have experience, but thank you for noticing." He said, "Let's see what I can do." And that's how I got promoted to dishwasher.

As a dishwasher I was so fast that the general manager promoted me to be a barback. I worked hard, lifting boxes, prepping, organizing, cleaning—it was a huge difference in workload compared to my job as a porter, but also in pay. And it was here at the Modern that I got my Spanish back. Because most people in the kitchen and behind the bar were talking in Spanish, and I got along with them well, but they were making fun of my accent and of me not understanding them. I thought, "This is embarrassing, I have to get my act together," so I took Spanish in college. (*Laughs.*)

At first, as a barback, I was nervous about going to the floor. I thought everybody was looking at me. I was so used to working in the kitchen and not being seen, but soon I lost this shyness and realized I could do this. I think my confidence came from the support of people who saw the good in me and gave me opportunities, especially my mentor, the general manager. He really invested in me, and when he went to a different restaurant, he took me with him. He often said, "I want the best for you." He didn't have to do that, but he wanted my success.

So, after two years at the Modern, I went to Craft, which was a very busy and successful place because its chef and owner, Tom Colicchio, was a celebrity, with his TV show *Top Chef* being one of the most watched shows at that time. I started as a runner, and in a period of two years, I got promoted to front waiter and then captain. I was twenty years old—I was the youngest captain that restaurant ever had. Suddenly, I was talking to all kinds of people—rich and educated people, celebrities, people who knew the restaurant world, and even to groups of twelve because we had two large tables at the front.

I had gained the necessary skills and confidence when I worked as a front waiter. At Craft, front waiters took the dessert orders, so I was a little bit behind the front line and could observe the captains. Each of them had their own style: the way they stood at a table, the way they made eye contact, the way they moved their hands. I took a little bit from each of them. And I was looking at the general manager, my mentor, observing how he acted: how he stood and watched everything, how he dressed. I served a lot and practiced, and when I got it wrong, I was thinking, "OK, that didn't sound right. How can I make it better next time?" I was always the toughest judge of myself. I always wanted to get it perfectly right—there was no room for error.

While I was working at Craft, where I stayed for five years, I got a second job at Momofuku Ssäm Bar because I needed to make more money. The chef, David Chang, who had also worked at Craft, was doing great things there and began [establishing] his legacy, so we were getting a lot of food critics and celebrities. For me, at first, it was a very different environment; it was all stools, seats with no backs, and the style of the service was different too. There were no tickets; you would just call the order out and needed to keep a mental count, and we had servers with piercings and tattoos. They would wear hats and shorts, but they were really serious about their technique. I picked up a lot there too.

That I became bartender at Ssäm Bar after being a captain at Craft wasn't a step back for me at all. Because at the end of the day, I want to own my own restaurant—that was always my goal and still is. So, I need to know how everything works because it's easier to understand people's frustration when you've gone through it yourself.

After some time as a bartender at Ssäm Bar, I got promoted to manager, which was my first management job ever. From there, I went to Charlie Bird and worked as a server again, even though they had offered me a management position. But I wanted to take it easy for a while. At Charlie Bird we had a lot of celebrities, regulars, and people from Goldman Sachs. The owners always had me wait on the celebrities, the regulars, and VIPs, and it was easy because I had six tables and performed what I had to perform, [took] the food order, [made] them feel good, but after a year I was ready for a change and more responsibilities. I needed new challenges.

I have a son who is eight years old and goes to third grade now. He eats well. He doesn't have to go to work. I love teaching him math and taking him out to restaurants. He has a lot of good in him, and he is always eager to learn and help. I will tell him everything I know as he grows older, and that it sometimes takes one good opportunity and someone to have faith in you to set you on the right path.

I always look back at how my uncle, who sadly is no longer alive, got me into all this by arranging that porter job for me at the Modern back then. I got so much out of it. And by working hard, learning as much as I could, and going to school.

School was a big thing in my life. I once asked my parents how far they had gone in school, and they didn't get very far. So, I knew that I wanted to graduate from college, that I wanted a degree, and I did. I always thought about the future, and I knew where I did *not* want to be. I didn't want to repeat history, so I knew I had to do the opposite of what was done before. That has always been on my mind.

My relationship with my father is great. He is now retired, and I am very thankful to him. I now understand why he was angry at me back then when I came back home without the jacket he had bought me. If he hadn't done what he did, maybe I would still be getting bullied. He conditioned me to this life, if you will. It took me a while to understand that.

CARLHA

I was born in the Dominican Republic, in a little town called El Rubio, near San Jose de las Matas in the middle of the country. I don't have many memories of my childhood in the DR, but I was a happy kid, and I do remember dirt roads, trees, beautiful rivers, lots of animals like cows, goats, and horses, and people growing their own fruits and vegetables.

My father was a fisherman. He tried to make a living fishing and searching for gold in the river, but it was just enough to put food on the table. He struggled so that we wouldn't struggle, but he never made it past the bare necessities. That's why he decided to come to the US illegally. It took him two years to gather the necessary paperwork to get us here, and to do so he married a friend of a friend in an arranged marriage. My mom had to get a visa and lived with an illegal status until I was eighteen because she and my dad never officially married. She couldn't go back for many years.

I was six years old when we came here. It was a big change for my sister, who is two years younger, and me. We came from the country-side—open farmland, lots of nature—and suddenly we were in a city with all these buildings and cars, in a country whose language we didn't understand. It was a total readjustment, made easier by the fact that we lived surrounded by other immigrants from the DR. We grew up in Washington Heights, which was like Little Italy and Chinatown, only it was a little Dominican Republic. (*Laughs.*) So even though it wasn't home, we lived with people who came from the same culture. It didn't feel that far away. And every summer, my sister and I went to the DR for a month or two, so there was never really a big separation from our country.

Living in Washington Heights was challenging, though. Not all people there shared the same vision, and many parents who worked hard to make sure their families had what they needed didn't pay enough attention to their kids. So, there were a lot of drugs and everything that comes with this . . . (*Fights back tears.*) Sorry, it's emotional. I just feel lucky that I didn't fall into that gap, where I would think, "Oh, my parents are not around—I'll just go hang out on the corner and start selling or consuming." That's the kind of environment Washington Heights was, and somehow still is, you know—an epicenter for drugs, violence, and things like that. I saw that very clearly. (*Fights back tears.*) Many of my friends from school and people from the neighborhood either ended up in jail or died from an overdose or a bullet. I made sure I stayed away from anything like that. I knew better. But it was happening all around us.

We were lucky; our parents were very present. Even though they worked hard, they were there for us with a combination of strictness, love, and understanding. They were always aware of what my sister and I were doing, what we were up to. And they made it very clear that they weren't going to let any of what was happening around us happen to us. That's not what they were working for, that's not why they came here. (*Fights back tears.*) I'm sorry. As you may already know, I'm a very emotional person. Even good things make me cry! (*Laughs.*)

Because my parents were working so much, I learned early how to cook; just enough to take care of dinner two nights a week when they had to work extra-long hours. It all began with rice. Surprisingly, it was my dad, not my mom, who taught me how to make it.

We were in the kitchen, and he explained, "You take a pot, heat it up, add oil, and put an equal amount of water to rice. For example, if you're going to use two cups of rice, heat up two cups of water with the oil and salt. Let the water come to a boil. While the water is boiling, rinse the rice, drain it, and then, when the water is boiling, add the rice and stir it on high heat. Let the rice soak up all the water. Once the rice has absorbed the water, cover the pot, lower the heat, and cook it for twenty minutes." To this day, that's still the way I make rice.

Then my mom taught me how to season stewed beans. After that she always had me helping in the kitchen, so little by little, my parents involved me in cooking until around the age of twelve, when I was able to prepare dinner myself. I mean, how many twelve-year-olds can do that?

Then one summer when I was fourteen, my sister and I started working. My dad has always worked in supermarkets as a butcher, and by then he was employed at a pretty good-sized store in Newark, New Jersey, where he commuted to six days a week. One day during summer holidays, he brought us with him and said, "Alright, I'm going to have you guys help out with the cashiers, and whatever tips you get are yours."

Three years later, one of the cashiers there said she was going to make a cheesecake. I said, "Oh, that's cool. Can I have the recipe?" She gave it to me, and I made that cake at home. It was so simple, but it turned out good, and people really enjoyed it. I thought, "OK, let's make some money then." I was seventeen at the time, and soon enough, I had a little cheesecake business, selling them to my coworkers. I'm not a cheesecake fan myself, but people kept ordering these cakes! At times, I sold up to twenty-five a week, all made at home. Later I started working as an usher at the Apollo Theater in Harlem and sold cheesecakes to my coworkers there. (*Laughs.*)

I've done a little bit of everything, and I absolutely loved working at the Apollo Theater. Oh my God, I saw so many shows there. A lot of musicals and, of course, Amateur Night at the Apollo! I worked there for four years, and my favorite musical was *Dreamgirls*. They ran it for over a month, and every time I watched it, it was a mesmerizing experience. It was such a beautiful show, and it was incredible to see the performers giving their all from start to finish, singing and acting with the same energy twice a day, seven days a week. I was in awe of their consistency and dedication. It felt like watching it for the first time every day. I truly admired that.

In between making cheesecakes and working at the Apollo Theater, there was also the Food Network, which I watched a lot. And more and more, when I had friends over, they wanted me to cook. I didn't go to culinary school right away. I tried college, but it just wasn't my thing. And I guess it was the appreciation my friends and family had for my cooking that made me think, "Alright, maybe I can do this for a living." The thing was, I had never set foot into a professional kitchen, despite working at McDonald's for a couple of weeks and later at Wendy's, but I guess that doesn't count. (*Laughs.*)

I went to the Institute of Culinary Education, which back then was still on 23rd Street. It was a great school with good teachers and classes, and everything else. The program was ten months because I didn't take any of the management or wine classes that were also available. I specifically pursued culinary arts. So, it consisted of these months and a 210-hour externship that I had to complete before receiving my certificate.

I did my externship at A Voce Columbus—that's where I met Chef Ayesha. She was a sous chef there. I had no idea what I was doing, but I fell in love with everything that was going on. Three weeks in, one of the garde-manger cooks was running late, and I was like, "What's going to happen? We're about to open for service, and the station is not set up!" So, I took out my notepad because I had everything drawn out and started setting up for service, even though I had never really worked the service before. Most of my duties involved prep, a lot of prep.

They had put me with the garde-manger team to help them with the prep. It was a very big station, and the cooks there were responsible for all their *mise en place* from start to finish. For example, there was a marinated bell pepper dish on the menu, so they had to grill, peel, and cut their own peppers. There was a lot of prep work involved, and they had shown me the setup and where everything went. I just felt like it was a sign, like I had to do it. So, when the cook didn't show up, I began setting up, and when the chef arrived, I explained the situation and what I was doing, and he was like, "Oh, thank you. Great job." Two days later, they offered me a full-time position and started paying me while I continued to complete my externship hours. That's also when Chef Ayesha started noticing me more. She was already aware of me, but now she really took me under her wing because she saw that I wasn't joking around.

She set up her station right next to me; we were working side by side pretty much the whole time. She would correct me whenever needed and show me what was right and what was wrong, teaching me how to be a strong woman in the kitchen, because that's tough. She always says that as a team, you are as strong as your weakest link. Meaning, you have to be stronger than strong because there will always be someone who is not at 100 percent, and you have to share some of your strength to help them out. And when you build that relationship with your teammates, they will help you out when you need it too. That's one of the things that has always stuck with me: always work hard. And being a female in the kitchen, you must work a little harder. It has always been my mission to prove myself as a woman in this industry.

I remember once when I started, I got sick and had to call out because I couldn't get up from bed. I was out for one day and went back the next day still feeling sick, but I knew I had to make a presence, being rather new. The chef pulled me aside into a walk and said, "My guys don't call out because they're sick." I said, "Yes, chef. Got it." It was this "my guys" that made me develop that thick skin. I always felt I had to prove over and over again that I'm "one of the guys," you know?

I worked at A Voce for four years. From there, I followed Chef Ayesha to Red Gravy in Brooklyn, where she served as the executive chef. The menu was all Italian, like A Voce, and at that time, I knew nothing about Middle Eastern food, except for what Chef Ayesha had introduced me to little by little. Red Gravy was located on Atlantic Avenue, which was a hub for Lebanese stores and restaurants. Chef Ayesha would bring snacks from these places for us and took me to these stores, introducing me to this cuisine, which she herself was so familiar with and enjoyed eating the most. But it wasn't until we developed Shuka that I truly began to comprehend the wonders of Mediterranean food.

She brought me here as a line cook, and I earned my spot as a sous chef. I had to start all over again, reading books and educating myself about this cuisine that I wasn't familiar with, and I'm still learning many things. Everything I know about it, she taught me, even though she says I taught her a lot as well, like patience, for example. (*Laughs.*) I think I've been a good enough student to be able to be the *chef de cuisine*, to run Shuka, and be a leader myself. And I have a very strong team, without whom this place wouldn't be what it is. It was a long way from

Washington Heights, and I'm proud I made it so far. And then there is my daughter . . .

She's three now, and she's my world, my everything. (*Fights back tears.*) Oh no, my emotions again! (*Laughs.*) I'm very grateful because my mom is still around, thank God—she helps me a lot with her. If she weren't, it would be difficult for me to balance both things, the job and the baby.

When I found out that I was pregnant, Shukette was in the works. It was clear that when Shukette opened, I would either go with Chef Ayesha or take over more responsibilities here at Shuka. I was super excited for both options, and then I found out . . . Well, obviously, it wasn't planned. And I was just like, "Oh my God, what am I going to do now? Am I going to lose everything that I've been working so hard for?" I kind of freaked out. And because of my personal beliefs, not having the baby wasn't an option. I knew I was going to have that child, whatever consequences that would ultimately bring. It was joy, but at the same time, panic and the thought, "Really Carlha, you could have waited." Then the pandemic hit.

I worked throughout my entire pregnancy. I had hoped to leave a month before my due date, but I ended up giving birth two weeks early. So technically, I was only out of work for two weeks. Thank God the birth was beautiful and without complications. I was strong. And when the pandemic hit, it was kind of a blessing for me because it gave me more time with the baby than I had anticipated. Now it's a matter of managing my time between work and home. I don't bring my laptop home and try to disconnect from work as much as possible. Some days are better than others, but I've been able to maintain a balance. If I can leave earlier, I will. If I must stay late, I stay. It's challenging, but I'm grateful for all of it.

I never imagined that this is where I would be. In my family, no one has a profession. People start something but never really finish it, or they finish but never pursue what they went to college for. I am the only one who pursued a profession that I went to school for, and I managed to stay in it, grow, and be successful. (*Fights back tears.*) And it's so much more than just cooking and creating new dishes. Managing a kitchen includes finances, extensive scheduling, planning, and team management. It's all these different aspects combined that make you a chef. And now that I am kind of running the show here, no one pulls me into a walk and tells me what "the guys" would do. Now, I'm the one who does that! (*Laughs.*)

MOHAMMED

I am from Gambia, one of the smallest countries in West Africa, with a population of two and a half million people. Gambia is home to about twelve different ethnic groups and at least thirteen different languages. I speak seven of them, and my ethnic group is Soninke. The official language in Gambia is English.

I was born in 1983 in Banjul, the capital, but I grew up in Serrekunda, which is about ten miles from Banjul. I grew up without my parents because they went to the United States when I was seven years old. They were here without papers, so they couldn't come back. They went to provide a better life for us. I was raised by my aunt, my father's sister. She was the best. Her name is Aisha. I named my daughter after her.

My parents did what many African immigrants do when they come to the United States: work to support their family back home. My dad worked construction, and my mom at a daycare in the Bronx. I didn't see them for twenty-three years, until I came to the United States in 2013; by then, I was thirty years old. That was the first time I had seen them since I was seven years old.

In those years in between, we didn't communicate much. Not every house in Gambia had a telephone, and there were no mobile phones yet. Only when people started getting mobile phones did we start communicating. And that's how we finally got reunited.

School life was good if you were living in the city, but it was a bit tough out in the countryside. That's where I started school, because that's where my family lived, with my aunt and her children. In 1992 there were no school buses for us. So, if your parents couldn't afford a bicycle for you, you had to walk. And not everyone could afford a bicycle. Later they sent me back to the city to continue my education there. But even though my parents sent money for my school fee, school was too costly, so I stopped after high school and did not go to college. In my country, not everybody can afford to go to college.

We didn't have access to the internet, and what people were telling us about the US was that it's a good country and one of the most beautiful in the world. We would see pictures, like of the famous places in New York, Times Square, the World Trade Center, and we thought every building there looked like that. Then, we started watching movies, and when we saw American films, we thought, "Wow, everyone is good in that country." It became everybody's dream to be in America. We all said, "One day I will be in America." It was only as we grew older that we realized that not everything about America is great. But when we were young, our imagined America was close to paradise. (*Laughs.*)

Growing up in Gambia, we didn't have a luxurious life, but we were happy with what we had. Most of my childhood friends are now in Germany, France, and Angola. When I talk with my best friend from back then, who now lives in Angola, we remember many things from our childhood. Like when we played soccer, but we couldn't afford to buy a real ball, so we rolled up some plastic trash in an old shirt until we had something that resembled a ball. Then we would play in the sun, barefoot. This is common in Africa. Most of the soccer superstars you see on TV all started out playing barefoot. Last year, when I went back to Africa, I saw some young kids playing like this, and I almost cried.

My aunt is one of the most beloved people in my life. I love her very much. I didn't realize she wasn't my biological mother until I was twenty years old. I've always called her Mom, and I still do. I found out accidentally. I was sleeping, and my aunt was talking to someone on the phone. I woke up in the middle of the conversation. She was telling her friend, "Mohammed is growing up, and someone really needs to tell him that I'm not his real mother. He's twenty now—he needs to know the truth." I didn't feel bad about it, though. I didn't know the story behind it. I pretended to be still sleeping so I could hear more of the conversation. My aunt's friend said, "Well, he's a man, and he'll figure it out on his own. We can't just tell him that." A few days later, I was still waiting for someone to tell me, but no one did. So, I had to ask my aunt myself.

My aunt is a very good cook, but her daughters are terrible in the kitchen. Last year when I went to Africa, I told them, "You still can't cook? Mommy is getting older, you need to learn!" (*Laughs.*) My aunt used to make this local food, which has many names, like *accra*, *pap*, or *benchine*. It is a porridge made from millet flour. We ate it every morning before school.

And then there is peanut butter stew, which you can cook with chicken or other meats, but the basic method is to let the water boil, set your peanut butter aside, and cook the chicken or meat separately. Once the meat is halfway cooked, you remove it from the water, add the peanut butter to the juice, and mix it until it slightly thickens. Then you put the meat back in and let it finish. It's one of the most common foods in Gambia; everybody loves it. Most people call it *domoda*, but when you call it peanut butter soup, everyone will know what you mean.

Gambian cuisine differs from the food of neighboring countries because of the many different ethnic groups with their own traditions and traditional foods. It is kind of weird, isn't it, with only two and a half million people? (*Laughs.*) But that is why many dishes from neighboring countries can also be considered Gambian dishes.

For example, *thieboudienne*, the national dish of Senegal, a flavorful rice dish cooked with fish, vegetables, and a tomato-based sauce. And then there is jollof rice from Ghana, a rice dish cooked with tomatoes, onions, peppers, and various spices. Some people even say it is from Nigeria. I don't know who owns it. And from Nigeria we have *fufu*, a staple food made from pounded cassava or yam and another standard of Gambian cuisine.

I have traveled to many countries in West Africa, like Senegal, Benin, Guinea, and Mali—all French-speaking countries. I went there for business trips, buying things and bringing them back to Gambia to sell them. Gambia is nicknamed as "the smiling coast of Africa" because it's known for its friendly people and as a tourist destination. We've never experienced things like terrorist attacks or rebel activities. It's one of the most peaceful countries in Africa. Ninety-five percent of the population is Muslim.

I grew up Muslim. My religion is important to me. It is who I am. It keeps me calm. The word *Islam* means peace. You cannot be a Muslim without being peaceful. And that is how I look at life. Whatever I go through, I believe it is from God. Whatever happens to me, I see it as my destiny. I do not see much difference between Islam and other religions. I believe what I believe, and I respect people who believe what they believe.

I went to high school in Banjul, our capital. Those four years were the best. I met friends for life; also, I enjoyed going to school. After high school, I didn't have a job. Back home, there are not many opportunities. It's not what you know but who you know that matters. You can graduate high school at the top of your class and still not get hired. But you might see some of your former classmates doing well, because they have connections that helped them get jobs. I didn't have those connections.

But one of my friends went to France and sent me 700 euros so I could start my own business. That was a lot of money! So, I went to Senegal and bought some lambs and goats and started my small animal farm. I also tried to introduce poultry, but it was too expensive and labor-intensive. Later, I got five cows. Then I realized that keeping cows is a lot cheaper than keeping goats because you only need to feed them once a day. So, I sold all the goats and sheep and bought more cows. I ended up with thirty-five cows. It took me about three years to get these thirty-five cows. I still have forty now. My dad takes care of them. When he retired, he went back home. My cows are giving me an extra income while I'm here.

I was kind of successful back then, but it still wasn't enough. The little I made I had to spend for living, even though life in the countryside is cheaper than in the city. Still, I couldn't save anything.

In 2012, three years before his retirement, my dad came to Gambia, saw my situation, and said, "OK, I have to get you to America." I answered, "How are we going to do that?" Because all I had in my name was thirty-five cows and my passport, and the passport was about to expire. My dad said, "We'll get you a new passport." By that time, he was legal in the US and could request a visa for me, and to get that he had to prove that he was my father, so we had to get a genetic test at the embassy in Gambia. The test was positive. I arrived in New York on July 1, 2013. Three weeks later, I got my green card.

I wasn't scared to come here and leave everything behind. By that point, I was happy to leave my country. I needed to start something new, something that would allow me to help my family and contribute to society. Also, back then our country was ruled by a dictator, one of the most brutal presidents in Africa. I didn't suffer directly from him, but it certainly didn't make me want to stay. I was eager to leave. And that's how everything started.

I was nervous when I came here because I had never met my biological siblings, my two US sisters. They were born here and grew up in the Bronx, but they know our culture and speak our language. So, when I met them, much to my surprise, I felt like they were from Africa; it was easy to connect with them. To come here and see my siblings like that made me very proud. African people in the Bronx teach their kids the traditions from their home countries, and that's why when you are in the Bronx and see an African kid, you feel like you are in Africa, just because of the way they dress and speak.

My first job here was as a dishwasher. I did that for six months and then I quit because I was only making six dollars per hour plus tips. I went looking for another job, and one day I was walking around with a friend at Union Square on 14th Street, and I saw a store where they made handmade cheese, on Broadway. They were hiring, so I went in. They asked me if I had any experience making cheese. I told them no; I had never made cheese in my life! (*Laughs.*) But I knew how to raise a cow and what good milk looks like. Well, they needed someone who knew how to make cheese, but they also had a kitchen, and for some reason they wanted to give me a job. They told me to talk to the chef. He hired me as a dishwasher for two months, then he started training me and putting me on the prep team, and so on.

I worked with them for three years. After that, I worked at Mastro's Steakhouse for two years. And after that, I ended up getting a part-time job at Upland, where I met chef Justin Freeman. I worked with him for a while. Then, all of a sudden, the pandemic came, and all restaurants were shut down. First, I did a little bit of construction. It was tough, too tough. I only worked there for two months. It wasn't for me. I can't do this. (*Laughs.*) One of my friends asked if I wanted to do Uber. I didn't have my driver's license, but he said it's easy to get one. So, I applied, took the driving test, passed, got my license, and worked as an Uber driver during the pandemic. One day I was chatting with Justin Freeman again. He asked me if I was interested in a job. And that's how I got to Cookshop.

It's important for me to go back to Gambia once a year to see my aunt, my wife, and my daughter. I got married in 2019. That was my first marriage. I got divorced and married again in 2020 and had my daughter with my second wife. My daughter's name is Aisha, like my aunt's. My wife's name is Penda. They both live in Gambia. I talk to them every morning before I go to work.

It's not easy that they are over there, and I'm here. It requires strength. But that's the reality for most African immigrants who come here, and you must have that strength to be able to support your family back home. Some of my friends in the US sleep four hours a day and work two jobs. It's a lot just to pay your bills here, and to be able to, on top of that, make money for your people back home. You often need a second job; one just isn't enough.

My dream is to start my own business back home; just keeping animals, developing my animal farm—that's what I'm planning to do. I will definitely go back one day. I don't know when, but I'm working on it. Luckily, I'm a citizen here, so I can come back anytime I want. I'm working on bringing my wife and daughter to New York. There is no real obstacle right now. Maybe there is a little bit of a financial issue, but I'm working on that. It wasn't my plan to raise my child here, but since I'm a citizen, it's an option.

JAKELINE

I was born in Lima, Peru, in April 1977. My parents separated when I was still in my mother's belly, and I spent only two years with my mother before my dad, who had better economic possibilities than her, took me and my siblings away with him. I don't know if my mother agreed to that, but he took us with him and raised us—or, well, his mother did. We didn't really see him much. We were four girls and one boy; I was the youngest.

We lived high up in the mountains. My father was a musician, so he was never home, and my oldest sister and my brother played the role of parents, along with our grandmother, whom I called Mom.

She was very strict. I learned at the age of seven how to make the bed properly and do everything else around the house in the best way. My grandmother's house had to always be deeply clean, and you had to get up early, brush your hair properly, and be well dressed in the first hours of the morning; otherwise, there would be no breakfast. My brother said it was like military service. (*Laughs.*) My grandmother demanded a lot from us and taught us things the hard way: how to be well-mannered, how to sit properly, and all those things that the old people found so important.

We had to be good and very careful with what we did and how we said things because everything had consequences. If we didn't bring good grades, we were not allowed to play, and she would tell the teachers not to let us out during the recess. If we did something not right, we wouldn't get a Sunday rest or food. That's how we grew up, but I loved her, and I still love her with all my heart.

I especially loved her cooking. When I was a little child, I would sit on the stairs of my grandmother's kitchen, from where I could see her stirring the pots, frying the food, and making the salsas. I would ask her everything about what she was cooking, why the salsa smelled so good and what she had put in it, and so on. I would watch and learn, but I never cooked with her; she wouldn't let me because I was too small.

She cooked all the time and knew how to make all types of dishes. Her best was green rice with chicken, ceviche, and *ají de gallina*. *Ají de gallina* is made with chicken breast in a yellow sofrito with a yellow chili from Peru, along with bread and milk. And when you put parmesan cheese on it, oh, it's delicious! (*Laughs*.) Her cooking left a lasting impression on me, like a stamp. And later, so did my mother's cooking.

I saw my mother again when I was eleven years old, the first time after we had gotten separated nine years before. I saw her, but I didn't recognize her; I didn't remember her. However, she had not forgotten me. She was so excited to see me; she hugged, kissed, and cried the entire time. In all those years, she had made a new life for herself. She had new children, a new family, and all that, but it didn't matter to her. She just wanted to have me in her arms and never let go. Maybe she never agreed to let go of me to begin with, who knows.

I went with her and started living with her and her new family. She made her money by cooking for weddings, baptisms, and birthday parties. She used a giant pot that resembled a huge water cylinder cut in half. Since she had much less money than my grandmother, my mom didn't have a big kitchen. She always cooked on the floor of her tiny house over an open fire of wood that she gathered from the forest. I will never forget the ladle of that giant pot. It was like a big broomstick and very heavy to move.

When my mother was hired to cook, I always wanted to help her. I just loved to stir the pot with that heavy ladle, imagining that I was the one being hired, that I was the one doing the work. Cooking made me happy. I was so happy to be with my pot and my ladle. I didn't know if I wanted to imitate my mother or my grandmother. I loved them both so much. My grandmother was hard, but she taught me a lot. I think I am here today and not starving because of the discipline I learned from her. My mother, on the other hand, was pure love.

She is from the south of the country, from Ica, which they say is the city of the eternal rising sun because all year round there is sun. There is so much fruit, especially grapes and therefore wine. That's also where the pisco sour [cocktail] comes from, and the *carapulcra con sopa seca*.

My mother's *carapulcra con sopa seca* was one of my favorite dishes. *Sopa seca* is a half-green noodle dish. You make a sofrito, add the chicken, then the noodles. *Carapulcra* is made from potatoes that are dried in the mountains. They dry them in such a way that they end up looking like beans. Then you cook them with a mix of wine, chili, herbs, and spices. The dish itself, when it's ready, looks like it's just beans with pasta, but when you eat it, it is divine. I love it because it represents my mother's land, it represents us cooking together, and it is something you only eat on special occasions.

That was my childhood. And when I had to go to high school, they sent me out of the mountains to the city, and that's where my [wandering] times began.

In the city, I decided to become a nun. I thought that was my vocation, but I was fifteen, still a minor, and to enter the convent I needed my father's signature, who didn't agree with my decision. He told me that if I became a nun, he wouldn't talk to me ever again. He said I would stop being his daughter. I loved my dad with all my heart, but I said, "I'm sorry, this is what I want for myself." So, I asked my mother and my baptismal godmother to sign the authorization letter I needed, and that's how I became a nun and lived inside the convent for six years.

I learned so much there. I learned even more about cooking, especially baking, and I developed a better taste in food. I don't know how long I would have stayed; I only left when I found out that my sister, who is two years older than me, had divorced, was left with a little boy, and was going through a very difficult time. I couldn't just stay in that convent and pray for her. I had entered the convent out of love, just like when you fall in love with someone and you're willing to leave everything behind for them, but I loved my sister more. So, I talked to the Mother

Superior and told her that I couldn't be there anymore. We nuns did a lot of social work, going to the mountains, to very poor places, and helping people in need in many ways, but the one person who I wanted to help most was my sister, and that I couldn't do from inside that convent. So, I left and went to look for her. I was twenty-one years old.

I arrived in the province where my sister lived, moved in with her, and quickly realized that with such a young child in her arms, she could no longer work. So, I decided to become the provider of the house and looked for a job that could support the three of us.

I found a bakery; the owner had a son who was a priest on the other side of the world, and when he learned that I had just come out of a convent, he welcomed me. He didn't ask me for papers or anything, and he told me that he likely would never see his son again, and that's why he would support me. I made coffee and helped him where I could, and on the side, I started my studies to become a nurse. For three years I worked for the baker, and when I was done with my education, I said goodbye to him and began to work as a nurse.

I worked at the hospital and took care of patients at home, but I was earning very little. I worked a day shift and a night shift, and I still barely made enough money for my sister, my nephew, and me to eat. I was also put in the care of dying patients, which was very difficult, because I always developed love for them, and then my heart would break every single time they died.

So, when I was twenty-five, I started working in the dollar exchange. Even though it was much riskier—many money exchangers got robbed or even killed—changing dollars was where the money was. If you were quick, clever, and trustworthy, you could earn well, and the commissions were in dollars. I was afraid, but with that work I could provide my sister and nephew with a much better life. I did this for ten years.

At the beginning, in my mid-twenties, I had a very small face, so people always thought I was only fifteen or sixteen years old. They liked me, saw that I was honest, and so I started to get clients. I worked in Gamarra, a commercial district in Lima and the largest clothing and textile market in Latin America. There, I independently bought and sold dollars and started to sell clothes on the side. I started to travel, bought clothes in Panama and sold them in Peru, but dressed in the cheapest clothes and sneakers possible. (*Laughs.*)

I had clients, store owners who trusted me a lot. One of them said, "This week I'm buying $20,000." She gave me the money in cash. I asked, "Madam, how can you trust me with so much money? I could just run off with it and use it to go to the United States." She laughed and replied, "Well, I'd hope you'd send me a postcard from there in that case."

It made me very uncomfortable to carry so much money with me that wasn't mine, but maybe that's why I was so effective at getting rid of it quickly. I bought and sold, bought and sold—I was very good. And so, little by little, people gave me more money, I became known, and I earned well. I was very proud to be giving my sister and nephew a proper life.

When you are working in dangerous things as a young person, you never think something is going to happen to you, until it does.

One day, I was trusted with $30,000 in cash. Right after I left the store and got into my friend's car, a motorbike stopped us. One guy put a gun to my head and asked me where the money was. They knew exactly how much it was. They shot the tires of the car, took the money, and left. How did they know it was $30,000 that I had hidden underneath my blouse? Who knows. It didn't matter; that store owner had trusted me, so I had to pay him back.

I cried a lot that day in my friend's car. How was I going to get that money? How was I going to pay the rent for that nice house I lived in with my sister and nephew? How was I going to pay for my nephew's school? What was I going to tell my sister? What was I going to do?

The day of the robbery was December 31st, and my sister and her son were waiting for me at home to celebrate the New Year together. When I arrived that night, I decided not to tell my sister what had happened. I knew that it was best for both not to know anything about it. I would just need to find a way to take care of them and pay back the robbed money. My sister noticed my sad face, but I shook it off, saying it was just a long day at work. In the end, I took out a $30,000 loan from the bank and spent the next two years of my life working to pay it back.

Two months after the robbery, I left for another town to look for work. Someone found me a job where I was supposed to sell wood, but it didn't work out. I returned home as a failure and finally had to tell my sister what happened. I also had to announce to her that we had to move to a smaller house. I was crying because I knew that the house we could afford would be one-quarter the size and in a poor neighborhood. My sister hugged me and said we would figure it out together. She started working and we took turns taking care of my nephew.

The new house I found for us was tiny, and so were all the rooms, except the kitchen. The kitchen was gigantic! (*Laughs.*) So, we spent most of our time there. We basically lived in that kitchen, so much so that we moved the TV from the living room into it. At Christmas all our siblings would come, and I would make each of their favorite dishes: soft roast with stew for my brother, rolled chicken and mashed potatoes for my sister, *sopa seca* with oven potatoes for my other sister, and anything with pork or turkey for my third sister. I always loved to be in the kitchen.

I gave myself to my family and didn't care so much about my personal life. My family was my priority and still is. And I am happy. But still, every now and then I wonder what would have been of my life if I had had more time for myself.

Once I had a boyfriend who was a commercial pilot and took me with him to Cuba, Panama, to Paris and Brazil. We never had the time to explore much because he had to fly right back, but I saw something of the world.

And then I almost had my own family . . . Once I got married, and I got pregnant and gave birth, but my baby . . . My baby died. I don't want to talk about it. (*Cries.*) Let's not talk about it . . . But my life lost meaning. Everything changed.

I couldn't stand the sadness of being in my hometown anymore. Everyone was constantly asking me about my loss, about what happened. Everything reminded me of it. I wanted to run away as far as I could and live in a place where nobody knew my story. It was unbearable.

I had a sister who was already in the USA. She couldn't have children, so she had her baby through in vitro. She told me I should go there. I had the illusion of being a mom again, but this time single and very far away.

So, I said to myself, "I'm going to apply to see if they will give me a visa for the USA." And they did. I was forty-one when I first went to the US.

A friend of mine was living in New York. I got a tourist visa that allowed me to stay for six months because she was getting married and wanted me to cook and bake for the wedding. I thought six months might be enough time to figure out a way to stay longer, maybe even forever.

On my first day in New York, my friend took me out to see the city. I was overwhelmed by the number of lights. She said I looked like a little girl on Christmas morning. (*Laughs.*) I wanted to sing every song I knew about New York.

The wedding turned out beautifully. Then, a friend of mine called saying that her sister lived in New York and was pregnant but not feeling well because she was lonely. She was due in two months but had been having pains for a little while. They were worried that her mother wouldn't make it in time to be there for her, so my friend asked me if I could check on her and keep her company, since I was nearby. I agreed, and then everything happened very quickly.

I was working in Brooklyn one night, taking care of a man's child, when she called and said she needed me now. She sounded troubled, so I called the man I was working for and told him I had an emergency. When he arrived, I took a cab to go to her. I was nervous because this woman had never had any prenatal care, any tests, or studies, so I didn't know what to expect.

When I arrived, I started talking to her. We did some breathing together, and I started to count the time to see how the contractions were doing. I was calming her down because she was very nervous and in a lot of pain. I could tell she was in active labor already, and the baby was very close.

I remembered my grandmother's secret for an easy birth: boiled wine with milk. My grandmother said that when you drink that, it warms your bones and helps you to dilate. So, I prepared it for her, and labor got stronger. We took a cab to the hospital, and I could see the baby's head coming out. She begged me not to leave her side, and I promised I wouldn't. She was very sad because the baby was coming earlier than expected, and her mother couldn't be there with her, so I tried my best and played that role. The baby came out fine; she named him Dylan.

I was there the entire time, and she was very grateful and now wanted to pay me. She said, "I know that you need money before you go back to our country." It was true because I had only found work babysitting that little boy at night and picking tomatoes briefly on a farm in New Jersey. However, it didn't feel right to take her money, so I told her, "No, don't pay me. I want to work before my visa expires and I must return, so if you want to give me something, maybe you could [connect] me with someone who needs a worker." She immediately said, "I have a friend who is a chef, and she works in a very good restaurant."

So, I called Chef Ayesha, and she said, "I'm sorry, there is only work for men right now. We are looking for a guy who can help in the back lifting the vegetable boxes and unloading the trucks." I said I could do that, so we arranged to meet. But when she saw me, her mouth dropped. She said, "But you're so skinny and short!" I replied, "I just need a girdle, and I can do it." And so, they hired me, and there I was, pushing and lifting and unloading boxes and sacks. (*Laughs.*) I was very happy to be working.

During this time, I met an Afghan man. He was American, but his parents were Afghan migrants. He was like a prince to me, and I fell in love with him. He was gentle, caring, and sweet. It was very easy to fall for him. I told him that I needed to go back to my country, and he said that I should go, renew my visa, and return as soon as possible so we could see each other again.

I left the USA, but we continued our romance through letters and calls. It was beautiful. I left in January, came back in April, and he immediately asked me to marry him. I thought I was living in a fairytale. He was handsome and gentle, and I thought there was no way I would find a boyfriend in Peru or anywhere else because I was already in my early forties. So, I accepted.

Communicating was funny because I don't speak English, but he spoke some Spanish and we always had Google Translate in our phones in case we didn't understand each other properly. (*Laughs.*)

They immediately took me back [at] the restaurant when I returned to the States, but my now-husband didn't want me to work anymore. As it turned out, his family was extremely wealthy. I didn't know it until after we married, but his family owned several stores, businesses, and properties in Manhattan. It started with him not wanting me to work, but besides that things were still fine. It wasn't until my visa expired that things turned around completely, and he became a monster.

The day my visa expired, he became a different person, and so did his mother. From that point on, they didn't want me to communicate with my family anymore. They didn't want me to have money of my own, and they didn't even want me to leave their home. I was a prisoner inside a big house by the beach. They took my phone away, and I lost track of time. He was unrecognizable. I didn't understand what had happened.

As soon as I could, I escaped the house and ran. I asked the next person I met. He took me in his car and [lent] me his phone. I knew the number of an aunt of my brother-in-law who also lived in the USA, but I didn't know where. She picked up, she said she lived in Washington State and that I could come to her. I didn't have a penny, but she helped me find my way to her.

This man—my husband, as absurd as it sounds—contacted me through my email and social media and threatened to have me deported. He said he would call the police and accuse me of having stolen from them. After our wedding I had received some very expensive jewels, which he said he would claim I stole. He threatened me in many ways and said things that scared me very much. I was especially terrified because I knew he had the resources to find me. I didn't know I had rights. I had no papers, no money, nothing.

The people from the restaurant contacted me and helped me to come back and get a restraining order. I immediately went back to work with them, but the restraining order didn't stop that man from following me everywhere. I was scared to death and imagined myself in jail, kidnapped, or worse. I cried and cried, but I didn't want to go back to my country, defeated, humiliated, and heartbroken. No, no, I wouldn't allow that. However, this time was the hardest and most horrible of my life.

His car was constantly parked outside the restaurant or outside my home. He spammed my email and phone with threats. I didn't want to live like that anymore. I couldn't. I even thought about the worst. The panic made me want to do things I didn't want, and so I ended up in a clinic. There, they helped me understand that what that man was doing to me wasn't right, and they helped me find more help. It was a long two-year process to pick myself up.

Work was my refuge. Chef Ayesha was always there for me; she even helped me find a way to get my papers straight and legalize my status. Through an organization that helps immigrant people, I realized I had more rights than I thought I did. I strengthened the restraining order because of the level of his threats, so now he is forbidden by law to find out about me through third parties, to look me up on social media, and so on. If I see him near me, I can call 911.

No woman should have to go through what I did with that man. Things I can't talk about. No woman, nowhere, never. I'm so glad it's all over.

It's been a few years since then, and I'm still working at the restaurant, which is my home, and the people there are my family. I call Chef Ayesha "Mom," and you—well, I never wanted to tell you, but when you're not there, I call you "Dad." (*Laughs.*) I love everybody at Shuka, and I'm so grateful for what you all have done for me. And look at me now, I'm working as a morning shift supervisor!

My sister, with whom I lived for those hard years in Peru with my nephew, is doing very well these days. She works in the real estate business in Peru and is very good at it. And my nephew is an engineer! Can you believe it? (*Laughs.*) He studied engineering in a university that is difficult to get into—it is only for very smart people. I am so proud of him. I go down there and visit them whenever I can, and then I make a big buffet with everyone's favorite foods.

Back in Peru when I was small, I always dreamed of having a café with a bakery, where I could make empanadas, *alfajores*, and other things. A small place with a warm and cozy atmosphere, a place where people could have a quiet cup of coffee and all that, Peruvian style.

Maybe I'll have that one day, maybe not. I am very happy with where I am currently, but maybe I can save up money and have that happen in my hometown because I could never afford it in New York. We'll see.

I came here with the illusion of becoming a mother again, but I guess at my age that's no longer possible. Maybe it is, maybe not. I'm at peace either way. I raised my big family with love, and now I want to travel. I want to know the world, I want to take long walks in different cities and fill my mind with memories—beautiful memories that I can look back on the day I leave this earth, so I know that I enjoyed my life and lived it well.

ISLAM

My name is Nurul Islam Lanin. My original first name was Muhammad, but when my father passed away, it was very difficult for me. His name was Nurul Islam, so I changed my name to Nurul Islam Lanin. I am from Bangladesh—Beanibazar, in the Sylhet district in the northeast of the country. My grandfather was a district leader and a religious leader, a very well-respected man. He passed away in 1966, so he never saw Bangladesh after it gained its independence from Pakistan in 1971.

We were a big family. I have four sisters and one brother, and on my father's side, I have eight uncles and four aunts. Everyone was getting married and having children, and the family was always growing. Before things got difficult, we all lived together, helping each other and always eating together. There were thirty people or more at our meals: siblings, cousins, uncles, and people who had worked for us in the fields for fifteen years or more. It was wonderful. But then, in 1988, we separated. It is a sad story.

I will make it short: Three of my uncles went to Kuwait to make money. One worked in a hotel, two in a factory. They brought more people from Bangladesh and made money with them by getting them visas. Another uncle was a doctor back then. So, the uncles were making a lot of money. Meanwhile, my father stayed at home taking care of the fields. We were a family of farmers, and as the second oldest, it was his duty to run the family business. It was my grandfather's land, and my father used it. Then two of the uncles came back; one opened a travel agency, the other a car business, and they moved with their families to the city. They didn't want anything to do with farming anymore. My father stayed in the village. Meanwhile, the uncles' families got richer and richer, really wealthy. And, you know how it goes, people become selfish. And then, in 1988, there was a big conflict about the land, and the family split. I was in the eighth grade at that time. In the end, my father was left alone with nothing.

I remember my father's face. He was so sad because he didn't have anything to feed us. So, he farmed other people's land and bought some rice, so we had food. It was the end of Ramadan, and my mother didn't have anything to cook besides the rice, so I went to the river and caught a lot of fish. My siblings and parents were so happy. I was helping my father wherever I could. I didn't have friends because I worked so much. Sometimes I cried. We had a water buffalo, some cows, and a small boat. I had to go three miles by boat to get food for the animals. Then I went to school. Most of the time I was the last person to enter the classroom. But I was happy to see my father's face when he smiled because I was helping. And I did well in school. In tenth grade, I was a science major. Really good.

Our family suffered for two years after the split in 1988. Our big family was no longer, but our neighbors helped my father. They used to call him "King." They loved him because he was always willing to help others. If someone asked him for money, and he didn't have it, he would borrow it from someone else to lend it to that person. Even ten years after he had passed away, some people paid back the money he had loaned them. He was a very well-respected man. That helped us to survive.

In 1990, two years after the split, my father wanted to send me to the Middle East to make money and help the family, but I didn't want to go. I somehow always rejected the idea of going to the Middle East. But a cousin of mine had gone to the United States and told me he knew a way to get me there. At that time, I didn't even know where America was. But I wanted to help my father. I was the oldest son, so I felt that I was the one who had to take care of my family. I was sixteen when I left; I didn't even finish tenth grade. The last thing my father told me was: "Always think and decide wisely. What is good for you, take it. What is not good for you, leave it, don't touch it." I have always remembered that.

Do you want to hear the story of how I came to the United States? I took a flight from Dhaka to Rome. From there, I was supposed to fly to Los Angeles, because I hadn't been able to get a ticket to New York. I had never flown before, so I didn't know how to transfer from one plane to another. But I saw a lot of Bengali people and just followed them. I thought they were going where I had to go. But they weren't. I spoke only very little English and no Italian and went to the counter and showed the person there my ticket and my passport. It was an older Italian. He looked at the ticket, then at me, and said, "You just missed it." It was a TWA flight. Do you remember those? And the next day after midnight, my visa would expire. He said to me, "If I transfer you to New York, you will be okay." He said, "Stay here until tomorrow morning, then talk to me." Then he left.

So, I stood there in that airport all alone, a sixteen-year-old boy from a village in Bangladesh. I tried to sleep on a bench in the cold. It was so cold. I was hungry, but I only had fifty dollars. I bought a Coca-Cola and a hot dog. I think that thing was a hot dog. I didn't know if it was halal or haram, so I took one bite and that was it. I couldn't eat more. Somehow it felt wrong. So, I only drank Coca-Cola until I had only thirty dollars left.

The next day, the gentleman came back. Big relief! I gave him my ticket and passport. He took me to a line, gave me a boarding pass, and said, "This is your flight. You're going to New York." I was so happy. I made a quick collect call to tell my uncle that I would arrive in twelve hours, and he said my cousins would pick me up. But when I finally arrived, nobody was there. They were all working. So I was at JFK, alone, with thirty dollars and no English. Luckily, I found this Bengali gentleman who was there to pick up his cousin. And he knew my father! (*Laughs.*) He asked, "Where are you supposed to go?" I told him my cousins' names and the address, and he knew them too. He lived in the same building, 32nd Street and 31st Avenue in Astoria! (*Laughs.*) It's a miracle, right? So, he gave me a ride.

It was a six-story building, and every day I went up to the roof and cried because I missed my family. After fifteen days, I got a job as a dishwasher at the Townhouse Restaurant on 58th Street. The chef was nice to me. He offered me $175 for six days a week. After two weeks, he raised me to $250. As a dishwasher back then, in 1991, that was not bad. After two months, I became a prep guy, so my salary went to $300. I was sending money home, I was buying clothes, everything was good—and then the chef left. A new chef came, a Spanish guy, and somehow, he didn't like me. So, I quit the job, went home, and cried again. (*Laughs*.)

After that, I worked in a Jewish deli on 39th and Third Avenue. I made baba ghanoush, tabbouleh, hummus, and sandwiches, and I also did deliveries. I made good money—good money. Like $600 a week. And this was a kosher deli, so Friday and Sunday you worked half days, and Saturday was closed, so it was almost like working four days. But somehow, after two years, the deli closed. It didn't survive. And then I changed my mind. I didn't want to work in the kitchen anymore because my roommates were making a hundred dollars a day working as busboys. So, I started working in the front of the house.

I gained some experience in a Japanese and a Lebanese restaurant until I found a good job at a restaurant called Veranda on 75th and Second Avenue. I started there as a busboy, then became a food runner, expediter, server, and bartender; but I did bartend only for two weeks because I didn't like the smell of alcohol and didn't want to drink it. I worked at that place for five years, until they got another guy, another server, an Italian. And they gave him forty dollars and me twenty dollars—cheap! I talked to the owner, but he didn't care, so I left and worked at Steinhoff Hotel for one year. Then I got injured. Oh, sorry, I skipped something . . .

You know, I always wanted to go to school when I came here, but I didn't know how to get in or how to register myself, and none of my people knew. And then I saw a lady in the train—I think it was 1995—sitting in front of me, doing algebra. I memorized the question, solved it, and wanted to go to school even more. So, I asked my neighbors, the white people, and they told me what to do. In 1996 I finally went, and three years later I graduated from high school. But I almost didn't! Because of my history teacher.

She told me to write an essay about Christopher Columbus, but I refused. I said, "You can ask me to write about anyone else, but I will not write about Columbus because I disagree with him." I still do. Back then, I had read some books and learned about the atrocities he committed against Indigenous people. I tried to explain my reasoning, but the teacher—she was kind of a mean woman—didn't want to hear about any of this. Columbus Day was coming up, and she was insistent that I write about him. I refused, and she failed me in the class, and I couldn't graduate.

To graduate anyway, I had to take the summer class, which was given by the dean. He gave me a test, and I passed everything, but he still insisted that I come to class every day. Of course, I was also working full-time. And to make things more interesting, I was still sleeping in the living room of the shared apartment, in front of the TV. So, I would come home after work at 2 a.m., trying to get some sleep before school, and then my roommates would come home from work—and often they wanted to watch TV. (*Laughs.*) Well, I made it and graduated in 1999 but injured myself before that. I was playing volleyball on the school team, and that's where I tore my ACL. So, I needed surgery, and there were some tough times ahead. But wait, I forgot something! The Clinton letter!

One day in my AP math class, we had to write a letter to Bill Clinton about the Monica Lewinsky thing. So, we all wrote and sent him letters, but I was the only one who got one back. I still have it, the letter from President Bill Clinton. In my letter, I supported him. I said that everyone makes mistakes, and that this had happened, but that he was doing a good job. He wrote back and said thank you, and I still have that letter. (*Laughs.*)

After high school, I went to college for a year and a half, while also working. But then 9/11 happened, and I was still undocumented, so I decided not to finish. Oh yes, I was there. I remember when the first tower collapsed. I was on Fulton Street trying to get away. I was driving in my car when this panicked gentleman stopped me and asked if I could give him a ride. I said yes, of course. He was shaking, and at the next red light, he jumped out and ran away, leaving the car door open. When I came to Five Points, where I worked back then—for twelve years altogether—I was exhausted and nervous. I still remember you giving me water. And I laid down on the couch, right?

I got married in 2001. That's how I became legal. Yesterday was my anniversary. My wife's name is Hafizah. She is from Bangladesh and came here in 1998. I met her here and we got married. After that, I was working, working, working. In 2004, we had our first child, our baby daughter, what a blessing.

In 2005, I finally went to Bangladesh and stayed there for two and a half months. At first, I didn't like it. It took me some time to adjust. Seeing my family helped. My father was still alive at that point, but he didn't recognize me. His brain didn't work anymore. Only on the last day, he said my name. He said, "Oh, he's here! Let's all eat together!" Then he started crying and jumped into the car, trying to come with me.

Eventually, I want to go back and live in Bangladesh. That's my plan. I'm still fighting for land. I went there in February for ten days. We have some cases pending, so I had to go. We also have a house that nobody lives in—it's getting torn apart. One day, I want to fix it. And when my daughter gets married, I'm going to live six months there and six months here. I'm going to live in our village, not in the city.

I have one daughter and two sons. They don't speak Bengali. This is my fault. I should have taught them. I tried to teach my middle son Bengali, but he said, "I'm not in Bangladesh, why do I have to learn Bengali?" I took them to Bangladesh a few times. They said they like to come to visit, but not to stay.

In 2014 I bought us a house, in Jamaica, Queens, and then we almost lost it. I closed on the house in March, and in June I tore my ACL again, same knee, another surgery. By then I was working at 54 Below, but because of the injury I was only working on and off, [on] average two days a week. I had a mortgage and, well, it was a bad situation. I struggled, but I overcame. I always believe in myself, and I always believe in God. He will not let me down. The trick is, whatever you believe in, you really must believe in it. You can't just go through the motions. You have to *believe*.

We are building a mosque. Right now, it's in my basement, but in a couple of months, it will be a real house. If you want me to, I will tell you the story. You know, I had a store here in Jamaica, Queens—an Indian grocery store. It was the first one to open, as there were mostly

African Americans here, not so many of my people. But I took the risk. The problem was that the area was a drug dealer zone, and they used to sell marijuana in my store. Yes, in my store. Two people would come in and just do it, and I couldn't say anything. I was afraid. So how did I solve this? I'll tell you.

So, while I had my second ACL problem and couldn't really work, I was building the store. (*Laughs.*) It was a tough shift. It took me three months, in between which I had the surgery. There was one leader here, a gang leader, a big guy. His name was Kelly. You know, every group has a leader. I was making a connection with him, joking with him, and playing with him. They still sold drugs in my store, but only when I wasn't there.

I had one employee who worked three days a week. I worked the rest of the week. One day, I got mad because I found marijuana in our bathroom. I called the police, a guy I knew, my detective with whom I had a connection from my time in Astoria. I told him what was happening and asked, "What are you going to do?" He said, "If you want, we can bring our cameras and everything, set it up, hide in the basement, and catch them in the act." I said, "No, this is not a good idea. I will get in trouble. But can you send some police officers to my store, just for a visit?" Two days later, two officers came, and I hung up a camera that didn't work, and a sign that said, "This camera is linked to the police department." Then I called the leader, Kelly, and told him, "Look, this is not personal, but they came in the other day. They said whatever I'm doing, whoever comes in, they're watching it. So be careful. I'm just telling you." And that was it. (*Laughs.*) Later, Kelly went to jail and called me a few times.

But the mosque, yes. I digressed. So winter was coming, and I saw people praying outside, and I felt so bad. The closest mosque was at least a mile away, so I set up a makeshift mosque in my garage and later in my basement. The congregation was mostly Bengali, with some African American and Yemeni people joining as well, totaling around one hundred people. I was the president of the mosque at that time, but I didn't preach to the people. We hired an imam for that. The community was growing, and I decided to buy a house in the area and turn it into a real mosque. That's when things got complicated, with many ups and downs, but we finally made it. I think our mosque will be ready in two or three months. Until then, people come to my basement.

Favorite Bengali dishes? Oh, there are so many! My number one is *shutki*, which is sun-dried fish with vegetables. First, you need to cut the dried fish into small pieces and wash it. Then we use onions, tomatoes, green chilies—the Thai chili or a special kind of chili we have called *naga morrich*. It has a wonderful flavor and is one of the hottest peppers on the planet. We also use *edo*, which is the root of the elephant ear plant. We use it in *shutki*. It's like a potato or similar to Jerusalem artichokes, but with a more aromatic taste. Additionally, we add some fresh fish to the dried fish, creating a stew-like dish. *Shutki*—that's my favorite.

My mother cooked that a lot, and our national fish, the *ilish*. It has an amazing flavor. It's also called *hilsa*, and it's related to herring but it's much bigger, weighing around three to four pounds. When it's fried with hot mustard oil, it's called *ilish bhaja*—a traditional dish that we especially ate during the Bengali New Year. But we had so many dishes. Before 1988, when the whole family was together and we had these big meals with thirty or more people, we would have six or seven dishes on the table. There would be some chicken or beef, at least one fish dish, vegetables, and lentils, but only the yellow ones. And you know *karela*, the bitter melon? We sauté it.

ROSIE

My name is Rosa, but to my friends and family, I am Rosie. I come from El Salvador, from a small city called Ilobasco that is known for its pottery. I came to the United States in 2003. I was nineteen years old when I left—[it was] right after I finished high school. I wanted to go to college, but I couldn't because of our economic situation.

To go to college, I would have had to leave home very early and come back very late. Therefore, I would have needed special transportation because our town wasn't safe due to the criminals and gangs. That's the main thing in El Salvador—the criminals, the gangs. If you live there, there are certain things you don't want to get into. You want to be far away from that stuff and people like that. And there were other things . . . Well, I don't want to talk about that. There were many reasons to leave. There was no future for me, at all. In many ways.

We were nine kids—I have four sisters and four brothers—and we lived in a neighborhood where my mom and dad bought a little piece of land and built a real house for us. Most people around us lived in metal shacks. If we didn't have a lot of comfort, they were worse off. From that time on, I tried to be grateful for what I have. We always had some bread, an egg, or a piece of cheese. I don't know how my parents did it, but I saw the difference between us and the others because we always had something to eat. When there was a storm or heavy rain, our house didn't get damaged or flooded like the houses of the other people did. I remember, after those rains, everything turned into water and mud, and when I went to school, I had to put plastic bags over my shoes until I reached the street. (*Laughs.*)

My mom used to work as a housekeeper, and I started working with her when I was eleven years old. She was working for this family who had two little girls. One day, their mom asked me if I wanted to stay with her kids while she was working, and she would pay me. I agreed, and I got paid. This family was very kind to us. The lady knew we were very poor people, and she just wanted to make us feel as good as she could. I always knew that there were many people poorer than us.

I never got involved with the criminals, not in any situation. We talked about stuff like that as little as possible, and never about politics. If it's bad to talk about politics now, it was much worse back then. You couldn't even get help from the people who were supposed to protect you. And if you did, they were probably involved with these . . . I can't even say cartels because I never knew more than what I saw and heard.

I lived in that neighborhood for fifteen years. And when I finished high school, I was ready to leave. I wanted to leave [long] before that, but I couldn't. My oldest sister went to New York in 1995, and I needed her help to pay for my trip. There was just no way I could have made so much money, and I worked a lot besides school. I thought I could save money, but it just doesn't work if you need money to buy food and support your family. And when my sister finally gave me the green light, I needed my mom to say yes to me leaving. So, to get her to do that, I told her: "Think about it—if I get there and work, I'm gonna send you money!" (*Laughs.*)

Where I come from, the land is tropical. We had coconut and mango trees. That's why I ate so much mango, and I still do. I used to climb those trees. The landscape was hilly, but the houses of the poor were low, and that's where the water went . . .

At ten o'clock in the morning, my mom and dad dropped me at the bus station. This was the goodbye. All I can tell you is I was happy. I was happy to leave. I was sad to leave my mom and dad, but the rest . . . I knew something better would come for me and my family. And it did, at some point.

At the border to Guatemala, we just showed our passports, and they let us in. The coyotes found us somewhere on the way in Guatemala. It's not you finding them—they find you! And they always do. My sister paid $6,000 for my trip. They got half in El Salvador and would get the other half in Los Angeles [when they delivered] me there. That was the deal. And that's the best way to go, with somebody who knows the route. Otherwise, it's very dangerous. I was lucky that I could cross the way I did, even though there were moments where I thought, "OK, it's over."

At some point, we were attacked by—I don't know who. We had just crossed into Mexico, and there was no house. We were in the middle of nowhere, and I remember just sitting beside the path with a group of women and kids. They were all from Honduras, El Salvador, and Guatemala. Suddenly, there were people with guns shooting, and everybody just ran. I don't know why they attacked us. Sometimes they belong to other coyotes and want to steal people from your coyote. It's a big thing going on between them, and you don't know anything. All you know is that you must run for your life. And that's what you do. We were women and children. We were supposed to walk in a line, and somebody who knows where to go was supposed to be in front. But when that happened, we just ran everywhere. Later, they came and found us. Because that's what they told us: "If something happens, you have to stay near the area where it happened." That they will come back. I don't know, but you must follow whatever they say, and I did. (*Laughs.*)

After that, they separated us, and later I was put in one of these big tank trucks. You know these trucks they transport gasoline with? It was one of those, but for water. We crawled into the tank through a small opening below. We were many people, we were in there like cookies, and we only had one tiny opening to get air—like three or four inches wide. And that little hatch at the bottom where we got in was locked. And there we were for maybe twelve, fifteen hours, yes sir. I can't say from where to where we went like this, but we had to pass certain areas where they had checkpoints, and it still was Mexico, and when we got stopped, nobody made a sound. I had no idea where we were when I got out of that tank.

Then we got separated again, and they put me and seven others in a big food truck. The front part of the loading space was sealed with wood, and that's where they put us. It was just a little square, and I don't know how they made us fit in there, but they did. They closed it and put some sacks with corn in front of it to show that they were just transporting produce, but the real produce was us! (*Laughs.*) Some people really suffered in there. Some were very scared, and one was complaining: "This is not what I was told it would be, and I paid so much money!" (*Laughs.*) Most of the truck was empty. There was just this layer of corn sacks as cover and then our box. Every now and then, we stopped at a checkpoint, and I heard the soldier asking the driver some questions, opening the truck, and knocking its walls, but it was all silly. They knew we were in there; they were paid. I was very happy about that. Because if they wouldn't have been paid, they very likely would have taken us.

All of this just to get us to the border, and that's where we crossed the desert. We walked from nine in the morning until nine at night. The actual border was just a fence. We were in Arizona now. They told us to keep walking, and then there would be somebody. By then, I was walking with maybe five people, two of them kids, six and eight years old, who I carried at times because they were very tired and exhausted. They were with their aunt, and I helped her.

Then we got into a minivan. They dropped us at these houses that had wheels. The next day I got picked up and they drove me to Los Angeles, to a shopping mall where my cousin met me and asked if I was hungry. I was. (*Laughs.*) I stayed two weeks in LA with my cousin to wait for my sister. She didn't want me to travel by bus because it was considered dangerous back then, and she didn't want to risk putting me on a plane, so she came from New York to LA to pick me up—in a bus! And it's not a short trip. (*Laughs.*) But she did it. And then we went to New York together. That was seventeen years ago, and I have never left the city since.

When I came here, I lived with my sister in Brooklyn and spoke zero English. My sister encouraged me: "The first thing you have to do is go to school and learn English." So, I did, and I think she even paid for it. She also found me a job, and it's funny—since that time I've been a server. My first job was here in Brooklyn in an Ecuadorian restaurant. It was a lot of fun. It was a very small place but very busy. That's where I got to know *caldo de bola*. Do you know *caldo de bola*? It's a soup of plantain balls stuffed with meat and veggies. It's very good.

I don't really miss Salvadorian food. You can find it here; you can find everything here, except for one fruit, *annona*. I miss *annona*. It's a very good and nice fruit. There are white and pink ones, and oh my God, I love the pink ones. Once they are ready to eat, they crack themselves open. But the food from El Salvador—honestly, that's not something I miss. I eat everything, all the foods in the world.

I worked for three or four months at the Ecuadorian restaurant, and then I left because the lady who was supposed to be my boss started drinking with certain friends in the dining room and often got very drunk, and I didn't know what to do. So, I left and started working in a Dominican restaurant where I learned how to cut a chicken into four pieces. (*Laughs.*) They also served alcohol there. I was told that I would just be a normal waitress, but then on the weekend they wanted me to dance with the people. Yes, dancing. Like, if a customer wants to dance with me, I have to dance with him. Right, I know . . . (*Laughs.*)

But that's something that happened and it still happens in Brooklyn at some places on the weekends when it gets crowded. But I never did it! Once they asked me, I ran away. I just didn't do it. I ran away and found this place in Brooklyn where I worked for five years. It was nice there because they didn't serve alcohol, only food. It was a Mexican restaurant, and there I learned all I know about Mexican food. After that, I went to your Cookshop, and here I am. (*Laughs.*)

Coming here at nineteen, not speaking English, I just dealt with whatever I had to. Thank God I had my sister, who had my back. Even though at some point it got annoying, because even when I was twenty-one, she would still watch over me as if I was a little girl. But that's how it is sometimes: you teach somebody to walk and then it's hard to let them run. Well, like I said, in life, I like to be grateful. And I think I should be more than that since my parents are here now. We are nine siblings, and seven of us are in New York, and now our parents are here too.

I know many people who miss their hometown, their country, and so on. Not me. I'm not saying that I won't go back. The day that I can do it, when I have the right papers, I'm sure I will. But then I will spend a week there, and that's it. That's all I want. (*Laughs.*) I was very young, and because of the lack of money, I never explored El Salvador. It's a small country, and I never traveled anywhere. All I did was go from my little neighborhood to school and maybe one or two times to the capital, San Salvador. I'd been waiting to leave since I was a little girl.

I waited for a very long time because the short life I had over there wasn't a pleasant one. Not at all. In many, many ways . . . (*Pauses.*) You know, since I was seven, I was sexually abused. It was very hard for me since it was a person very close to me. Super close. A person you trust. A person . . . Well, at the end of the day, I realized that most cases are like this. The person who is closest to you is the person who does that to you. At some point, I was eight or maybe nine . . . Can you imagine an eight- or nine-year-old girl crying at night because . . . (*Cries.*) And unfortunately—you try not to blame people, but at the end of the day, you get angry and upset with things, and you do blame people, but I'm trying not to. I try to be grateful. That's the way I've been surviving without any therapy.

Laura, my younger sister, knows and of course Marivelle, my older sister, the one who brought me here. They try to understand me in many ways. Back then in my old life, I was struggling because of what happened. When something like this happens to you, and you are at school, it is very hard to be good at school. And as a little girl, what can you do? You need an adult who helps you, but I didn't have that support. And that's why I say I'm not gonna blame my mom. Because for me, my mom is a hero, in many ways. But in that way, she fell off. She couldn't . . . She didn't do anything about it. She knew. She knows. Of course. But she did nothing. If not even your mom is supporting you . . . And who is gonna believe you anyway? You know what I mean?

Yes, of course, it was my dad. And can you believe it that after all that, we brought them here? We brought them here because of what? Well, because they are our parents, that's why. And because I started to believe that it's not my fault. Because I started to believe that, at the end of the day, he is the only one who gets hurt by himself for all the things he did. (*Cries.*) So my mom couldn't do anything, and now—we just couldn't leave them alone. We couldn't leave them there on their own. Maybe I could do that. I could say, "You know, cut everything," but . . . He's a human. And I'm not going to do to him what he did to me. (*Pauses.*) How was I able to bring them here? How? Maybe because the only reason why I'm in this world is because of them. They made me! God used them to send me to this world. That's all they did. Yeah. And now I have this life. Which is mine. Not theirs.

What made me survive is God. I believe that He is the one who gives me the strength to survive every one of those single moments that I can remember from that time since I was seven years old. And of course, you could ask, and I, too, have that question in my mind: Where was He when all this was happening? Today I sometimes don't even know how I did it back then. But also then, later, He had so many good things for me. Like all these people I've found that helped me in so many ways. People who have told me or made me feel, "You can't stop—you gotta go on, you have to look forward and move on." In New York, I've found people who appreciate me as a person because when you feel like your value is nothing, you . . . (*Cries.*) You see, I can't even talk about that without those tears coming out. Sometimes I feel like I cried them all out, I don't have any more, but they always come out. (*Laughs.*)

So, I can say, I don't have that home. I don't miss my life over there. It was easy for me to leave all that behind. To come here, to find this place and really like it, to learn all I did, and start living the life I do live now. And the trip that I had from El Salvador to here—believe it or not, for me, that was an adventure. Even though it was hard and at some points I thought I wouldn't make it. But I did make it, so . . .

What I feel for my parents, in Spanish, we call it *lastima*. Pity. I feel pity for them—for my dad, for what he did, and for my mom, that she didn't have the strength to say or do something about it. And at this point in our lives, seeing them in this city, helpless, without knowing anybody . . . We brought them here because we all said, "They are our parents, we can't leave them there and let them die in misery, we can't do that." And so, I did my best to have the strength to deal with them after all that. I guess in the end, what they did to me made me find my strength. Something needs to be exchanged, don't you think so? Yeah, something needed to be exchanged. That's the way I see it. That's how I try to deal with it. Because I have to bring him to the doctor. I have to bring this man to his doctor's appointments . . . (*Cries.*)

OK, sorry, that all just came out. I think I needed to talk with somebody to find a way to . . . You know, I'm looking for a therapist, but I don't seem to be able to find one, because . . . I'm scared. I'm looking for one but at the same time I don't know, should I really do it? But I think I need to. Every time these feelings come up in me, I feel like I need it . . . I just can't keep them in that room anymore. There is a room inside of me where they are, and if I open that little door, they come out and hurt me. That's why I am scared to open that room. But I need to clean that room out. Until now I was a *cajita*. Do you know that word? It means little box. I was a little box. (*Laughs.*) But not anymore.

MASSOUD

My name is Oscar. I am from Ivory Coast and Burkina Faso, and I arrived in the United States on December 14, 2014, with a student visa. I was going to Temple University in Philadelphia but quickly couldn't afford it anymore. The language program alone was $6,000 per semester. I kind of knew it beforehand, but I thought I could figure out a way to make the money. Well, I couldn't. So, I transferred to the American English Institute in Times Square in New York City where my brother had been living since 2012. My plan was to learn English, work, make money, and then go back to college. I was twenty-five. And that's how the journey started. (*Laughs.*)

I made a friend at the language school who told me to go to Cookshop and ask the chef for work. When I arrived, Chef Andrew asked me, "What do you want to do?" I said, "I just want a job." He took me to the dishwasher station. "Well, this is your workstation. You will clean the dishes and bring them to the kitchen. When can you start?" I said, "I'm ready."

But there was a problem. I didn't have the necessary papers to work, only my student visa. This is of course the common issue for immigrants in the United States. You need to get some kind of work permit. My brother helped me. He said, "I asked a friend of mine. You can use his papers to work. There's only one thing," my brother said. "You have to use his name." So, I started working under the name Massoud. (*Laughs.*)

My journey really started here at Cookshop. My time here was something that really built my foundation as a person. I worked as a dishwasher for three months, but I had to pay for the language school, and I wasn't making enough money. So, I went to Andrew and said, "Chef, I need to make more money." He said, "You can do the prep downstairs." I replied, "Yeah, but still, that won't be enough to help me with my school. I want to be on the floor." So, I got a job as a busser. I was good at it. I worked very organized and fast; everyone else on the team kind of followed my lead.

I don't know from where I got this approach to work. Maybe it has something to do with my time in boarding school. As a kid, I was sent to a boarding school for four years. It was one of the best schools in my country, a school for the rich. I got there with a scholarship; my parents were middle class, a rare thing in Burkina Faso, where you are either rich or poor. The whole concept of the middle class comes down to how you manage yourself to be a little bit outside of the poor circle. So now, in boarding school, I was dealing with rich people. I would see them getting things or buying things with the money their parents gave them, while I had to make do with a limited budget. I think that's how I learned to manage my money, stay organized, figure out what I want, and be focused on achieving it.

My childhood was split into two parts. I was born and raised in Ivory Coast, in Abidjan, the capital. There I went to primary school until 1999, when the political crisis erupted. My father was a medical doctor and always working. My mother took care of the household and us: my sister, my brother, both older than me, and me. My parents were from Burkina Faso, a country we kids only knew from our summer holidays. And now people in Ivory Coast turned against people from Burkina Faso.

The problem was that people from Burkina Faso owned a lot of land in Ivory Coast. They worked the land as farmers and sent the money back to Burkina Faso. This frustrated many people in Ivory Coast, who had less land and made less money. I was eight years old and aware of what was going on because my dad had made it my duty to watch the evening news every day, so when he came home from work, I could tell him what was happening in the country. So, I knew what was going on and that I might not be able to go to school anymore, and I decided.

I don't know how I made that decision; I was just a kid, but I did. I asked my father if I could live in Burkina Faso and go to school there. He agreed. And that's how my brother and I were sent to Burkina Faso. My parents stayed back in Ivory Coast with my sister.

We moved to Bobo-Dioulasso, the second largest city in Burkina Faso, where we stayed with my mother's sister while the crisis in Ivory Coast worsened and became extremely dangerous. People from Burkina Faso and other African countries were being hunted by death squads. Fortunately, my father was well known and had many friends in the government, the police, and the military. One day, one of these friends called him and said, "Listen, you have to leave the country today. They're coming after you tonight."

One of the airlines there, Air Burkina, had a chief who was also my father's friend. My father called him and asked for a seat on a plane. There weren't any available, but because my dad had been working for the airline, they got him one at the very last minute. Later, my father told me that he was still scared even at the airport, before he boarded the plane, fearing that they might come and pick him up and take him away.

That same day that he left the country, the authorities took my mother and my sister, who was pregnant at the time. They took them to the headquarters and questioned them, asking where my father was. My mother told them that he had left for Burkina Faso, but they thought he was hiding somewhere and held them for three days. They released them only after my father called one of his friends, who was a chief in the Ivorian army. They were really shaken after this.

I never thought of leaving my country. It was my brother who had always wanted to go to Europe or the US, and in 2012 he left for New York. I wanted to stay in Burkina Faso, go to school, get a job, and work for NGOs. That was my dream: to help people. But after graduating from college, I felt the limitations of my country. On a bulletin board, they posted the names of people who had been accepted to university. On the first day, my name was there. The next day, it was gone. Corruption is a big problem in Burkina Faso. To get into higher education or a good job, you need to pay money or know someone who can help you. We didn't have either of those things. So, I was left out. It was frustrating.

When my brother came to visit, he saw my struggles and tried to convince me to come to the US. My dad thought I should follow my brother's lead, and at some point, even my mom thought it was best for me to leave. She said, "Go stay with your brother. The two of you can better support us that way." So, I said to myself, "If that's what I need to do, I will go."

That I then ended up washing dishes was very important for my life. Of course, going from Temple University in Philadelphia to washing dishes in New York City—that wasn't planned! (*Laughs.*) But I think I had to go through that to become who I am today. Washing dishes revealed a side of myself that I wasn't aware of. I was working, but I was also having fun. In the back of the restaurant, everyone knew me for singing and dancing while washing dishes and mopping the floor. For me, it wasn't just a job I had to do to survive. I knew I was making something of myself. I knew who I wanted to be and where I wanted to go, and I did my best to get there.

So, after working as a dishwasher, I became a busboy to pay for language school, and six months later, I was trained to be a barback. I was doing well, and the bartenders loved working with me because I kept the fridge organized. (*Laughs.*) I was always up and down the stairs, making sure they had everything they needed. We had a lot of fun, and after a year and a half as a full-time barback, the manager asked me if I could help in the kitchen, so I became a food runner. I had to hold hot plates and learn how the kitchen works, a totally new environment. It was tough, but I was learning fast. Soon, I was one of the fastest on the floor. I faced a lot of issues in the kitchen, though. I was the new guy who had come in and done so well in such a short amount of time, and, well, there was some pretty blatant racism too. I don't really blame them, though, because I think that's the society we live in. My way of dealing with this was to work harder and show them that no matter what they did, I wouldn't be defeated. I worked for myself and for Cookshop, not for them.

And then I decided to pick another path in my life. I left Cookshop and started driving for Uber! (*Laughs.*) I don't know why I did that. I think it was because my brother drives for Uber, and he was making good money. He still makes good money that way. So, I quit my job, waited two weeks for my TLC* license, rented a car, and in my first week, I got two tickets that cost me six points on my license. (*Laughs.*) Some customers were very nice, some were very mean. I made $13,000 in only six weeks, but I quickly realized it wasn't my thing, so I looked for something else and saw an ad for a job as a car salesman at City World Hyundai in the Bronx.

I met the general manager for an interview and told him everything I knew and everything I wanted to achieve in my life. He asked me one last question: "Where do you want to be in five years?" I said, "With all due respect, sir, five years from now I want to own your seat." He said, "I'm not mad at you. That's what you want. And you know what? I'm going to hire you." I was a bit shocked, because I didn't know anything about selling cars. I started working there in February of 2019. Three months later, on April 29, 2019, I got married. My wife is from Antigua in the Caribbean. And if you can believe it, we met on a dating website. (*Laughs.*)

I worked at City World Hyundai for four years. I was a salesperson for a year and a half, then I became a sales manager, managing a team of eleven salespeople. I worked from 9 a.m. to 10 p.m., getting home at 11 p.m. or midnight because we live one hour away from New York City, in Brewster, upstate New York. We bought our house in 2020 during COVID. I took all my savings and gave them to my wife. "This is all we have," I said. "Let's buy the house. We'll work hard and make the money back." And that's what we did. In less than five months, I made back all the money we spent on the house. We even did some renovations. We have over $100,000 in equity. Sometimes you just have to make decisions and see what happens. And if it doesn't work out, you learn from it.

Well, you wanna know something? Last month, I quit my job. It was time to move on. But before I quit, I went to Africa to see my father.

My father had been sick for a while. I'll tell you more about that later. It's a crazy story. But I said to my brother, "He's sick and getting

* Taxi and Limousine Commission

old. Let's take a trip." So, I bought plane tickets for him, my wife, and myself. With everything I spent over there, it was an expensive journey. (*Laughs.*) But it costs money to go back home because there are many people who need your help. It didn't bother me, though, because I felt I was doing something good. We visited my dad in the hospital, and it was great for him to see all of us together. It helped him recover quickly.

One thing I was able to achieve, thanks to my work as a sales manager, was buying a house for my parents. My brother and I bought it last year. The neighborhood where the house is located has no electricity, so I installed solar panels. I renovated the whole house, put up security fences, and installed a doorbell. This is not a common thing in that area, but I wanted my parents to be comfortable. I think they deserve it for all they have done for me.

My father came home from the hospital two weeks ago and is still recovering. He will need another six months to a year to fully recover from his wound, but he is doing well. So here is the story:

My father had a small wound on his big toe that did not heal properly. He decided to go to his village to get better treatment, which turned out to be the biggest mistake of his life. The wound worsened, spread to his knee, and became infected. We had to get him to Mali for treatment, and we organized everything from here.

First, we faced some problems with his brothers in his village, who did not want to let him go. On top of that, the security situation in Burkina Faso was very unstable. The village was cut off from the capital due to terrorist activities. Most people had left the area because of the killing and looting, and the village was in the middle of this conflict, so there was no ambulance to come and pick him up. We had to pay someone to take the risk and drive him to Mali. It worked, and my father spent three weeks in Mali. Then we hired another car to take him back to Burkina Faso.

In Ouagadougou, he went straight to the hospital. We have a cousin who works there, and he helped with finding a room and getting the best surgeon in the hospital to take care of Dad. He had to be taken to the operating room the day after he arrived. He had lost so much blood;

they had to give him blood transfusions. Then they cut the flesh from his leg, from his knee up to his little toe, to clean everything. The other option was to amputate his leg. Before they did it the doctors asked my mother, "Do you have the money to pay for all this? Because that's going to cost you guys a lot of money." She told them, "Don't worry about the money. My kids are living in the United States. They will pay for it." (*Laughs.*)

One of the things I enjoy when I go back home is the food. No matter how hard I try, the food I cook here doesn't taste the same. Well, maybe sometimes I get a decent *riz gras* or *babenda*. (*Laughs.*) That's one of the main dishes in Burkina Faso; my mother used to cook it a lot. It's made of beans and rice, cooked together with oil and spices, a hearty meal that can keep you going until dinner time and a popular food among people who work hard in construction. From Ivory Coast, I love potato leaf stew, a popular dish that's made with potato leaves. People wash the leaves, cut them up, and fry them in palm oil. Then, they add beef or lamb, along with some spices, and cook the stew for about one and a half to two hours. It is typically served with rice.

In Burkina Faso, people eat a lot outside, often food cooked by street vendors, like *poule flambé*, grilled chicken, a popular dish. You sit outside, grab a beer, go to the guy who runs the grill, point to the chicken you want, and he will cut it into small pieces, give you some spices on the side, and you enjoy your chicken, drink your beer, and you're good to go. Another classic Burkina Faso dish is called pork fufu. In the morning, they put a whole pig in a brick oven and cook it for three to four hours, so it's ready around noon when people have their lunch breaks. People eat their pork fufu, maybe with a beer, and then go home to take a nap before returning to work. (*Laughs.*)

I am hopeful about the future of West Africa, but it is still a long journey. The fight against terrorists—who no one knows where they get their money from—is a big problem for all the countries in the region, and it will take some time to fix that. No, I have no desire to go into politics there. In Africa, that can cost you your life, and if you are not part of a certain group in society, you will not get very far anyway.

But I have a dream to enter politics in the United States when I become a citizen. Right now, I have a green card. But I really do want to get involved in politics here because I feel like there is room for improvement. And I do believe the underrepresented need to create a new dynamic that will help people see this country in a different way. I believe the change must come from every single citizen and every single immigrant that comes to this country and achieves success. People say the American Dream doesn't exist anymore, but it does. It just depends on how you perceive the situation and how you make your way to that level of achievement. But I will say this: in life, luck sometimes exists. You need to have luck to be able to achieve certain things.

I am thirty-three years old, and I came to the United States when I was twenty-four. I never imagined that I would be able to make the kind of money I am making now. If I converted my income into the currency of my home country, I would be rich. However, the system here does not allow you to really enjoy your money. One-third of your income goes to taxes. Last year, I made a quarter million dollars, and I paid about $70,000 in taxes. I do not mind paying taxes, but I do believe that we should use more of that money to help people in need.

And we need to teach people how to use their credit cards. If you know you can't afford to pay it off, don't use it. But the system is built in a way that you need credit to buy a car or a house. And I think that's what's damaging the foundation of the young generation that is coming up, who want to flourish and become a better generation. So, I think there's a lot of work to do. A lot of work.

I don't think I will move back home to Africa. For me, wherever I make my money, settle down, and build my wealth and my future, that's where I belong. That doesn't mean that I deny where I'm from, but I'm proud to be here. And I won't mind being called an American. When I came with my student visa in 2014, they asked me many questions at customs. "What are you here for?" "When will you leave?" The first time I left the country and came back with my green card, they said, "Welcome home." *Welcome*—to me, that's a very important word.

I just started working for Genesis, the luxury car brand of Hyundai. It has been an interesting journey so far, but I don't dwell on it too much.

I'm always focused. I make decisions, I take risks, I have a very strong work ethic, and I'm working hard on myself because I always want to make sure I do my best. I do believe that you must do what is best for you. And the only person who knows what is best for you is you. And if you fail, you are going to learn from it, right?

JENNY

My country of origin is Colombia. I am from Bogotá, from the capital, and I lived most of my life there. My mother is from Neiva, a town seven hours away, but she left with her parents and her many siblings to Bogotá when she was a child. My father never cared about me; I only met him once briefly when I came out of school. I was in ninth grade. My mom has been my everything, my everything always. She worked on the street as a peddler, selling books and sandwiches to passersby. Whatever there was to sell, she would sell.

Every day I would get out of school and go to my mom's stand, and one day she was there with a man. She told me, "Jenny, I introduce you to your father." He was a tall man, and he looked just like me, exactly like me. We both immediately noticed we had the same moles on our nose and around our mouth, all our features looked the same, and I am also very tall. So, I kept looking at him and said, "Ah, nice to meet you," and that was it. The first and last time I ever saw him, the first and last words we ever shared. I remember that when that man saw me, he opened his eyes very wide, and tears ran down his cheeks, maybe because we looked so alike, or maybe because he never even threw a piece of bread in my direction.

My mother had to carry the weight of raising and caring for me and my siblings all on her own. And I thank God for my mother. That lady gave me an education—she has helped me so much, so much. I am very grateful to my mother because, despite everything, she got us through as best she could.

My mom got together with another man when I was two years old, so this other man practically raised me. When I was eight, I remember he one day tried to punch my mom, and I immediately got involved. I was small, but there was no way I was going to allow it. She tried to stop me, but in that moment, defending her, I was unstoppable. My mom is my mom, and nobody touches her. That was the last time he ever tried to hurt her in front of me.

I used to call him "Dad" when I was younger, but later he started to see me not as a child anymore but as a woman. And he, well . . . He tried to go overboard with me. He would tell me, "Don't say anything. You can't say anything because they won't believe you." He said other things too—it scared me. I was ten, maybe eleven years old. At the beginning I didn't say anything, but then I thought, "Why do I have to keep quiet if this is not right? He's touching me and I don't want that." So, I decided to tell my mom, and she said, "This will never happen again, I'm stopping this." And she left him. He tried to prevent it. At some point he was even hitting us both, but my mother said, "No more, no more—let's go."

Two or three years later, he got very ill with stomach cancer. He was the father of my younger brother, so he was in a way still part of the family. I never went to see him at the hospital. They told me to go, but I didn't want to. I really didn't want to see him. They insisted and I never went. And then one day they told me he had died, and much to my surprise I cried and cried and cried. Even though all that had happened. It gave me so much pain that he had died. I think because I also experienced many good things with him before it all happened, and because in a way, he raised me, I guess. I swear it hurt me—it hurt me too much.

I went to his cremation. I was there with all my nephews and my younger brother, and he was lying there, dead. They were putting him inside the oven, and for a moment, I swear I saw him open his eyes and quickly close them again. I started screaming, "He is alive! He is alive! Don't burn him yet! Believe me! Look!" But, of course, they just continued. Shortly after, a friend assured me that I wasn't crazy. She explained that this occurred when the deceased wanted to take someone with them. I thought, "Of course, it's going to be me. He's taking me because I didn't visit him in the hospital when he was sick. He's taking me because I never forgave him for what he did . . . But no, I don't want to die."

Things began to make sense when, a year later, his youngest brother passed away. And I realized, "Oh, it wasn't me he wanted to take along— it was him." I felt so relieved. This was when I was about thirteen or fourteen years old.

His family loved me a lot; they had made me part of their family too, since I was very small, as if I [were] blood of their blood. So, I told them, too, what had happened, what he had done to me. He was wrong; they believed me, they helped me.

In the years to come, my mother fell in love again, but that person hurt her, betrayed her, and so my mother said, "No more. I don't want to have anyone anymore. I don't want to love a man ever again." Maybe that's a very ugly thing to say, but it is also good.

I finished school and started working as a technology media operator, taking care of security cameras and things like that. But the situation in Colombia is not good, not good at all. You must have a lot of contacts to be able to have a good job. Because if you don't, they give you whatever there is and pay you almost nothing, and neither me nor my family had any contacts.

When I was twenty, I fell in love with a man, the father of my oldest daughter. It was a very toxic relationship, a long ten years of beatings, physical and psychological abuse. Whatever job I found, he would eventually always come and make scandals in front of everybody, yell at me, beat me in front of people, and so I never lasted long in any place. I would file legal complaints against him, one, two, three, multiple times. But the law in Colombia is terrible, and they always forced me to reconcile, to forgive him "for the child." And he also forced me to drop charges, threatening me. He told me that if I did not forgive him, that if I did not go back to him, he would kill my mother and my brother. He said that he would kidnap my daughter, and I would never see her again. So, I filed several, several complaints, but I always had to drop the charges.

We each lived in a rented room on the fourth floor of a building, each paying our own rent. He had a liking for beating me up and locking me in that cramped room on the fourth floor, refusing to let me leave. Nearby, my mom had rented another room. From my window, I would shout to her, seeking help. To prevent this, he covered the windows with tape, making them impossible to open, but he forgot to tape the upper one, the one highest to the ceiling; perhaps he thought I couldn't reach it. But when things got too horrible, I found a way to reach that window and yell to my mom for help, asking her to call the police, to do something to help me.

The last complaint I filed was because he went crazy and didn't care that our daughter was there, seeing it all. He beat me so badly that he broke my eye. He truly went crazy. I started screaming in fear and my daughter screamed with me. It was a horrible thing. I went back and filed a complaint against him, but this time, despite the law trying to convince me to "make amends with him" and despite his threats, I did not drop the charges. I told him, "No more. No more."

Because of everything that was happening, I was evicted from the room where I lived with my daughter on the fourth floor. They put all our belongings outside, and I had to go somewhere else. I did, but he always managed to find us. He would break down the door and windows to get in. No matter where we hid, he found us. This guy was crazy, in a horrible way. Horrible.

Even though we weren't together anymore, he was such a possessive person and so jealous, even though there was nothing to be jealous about. It was just me and my daughter. I was already on the verge of madness because I was so afraid all the time. I felt like he was going to break in again and hurt us. I was scared of everything. I couldn't sleep at night. It was horrible.

He eventually found me. I was with my mother and brother. He found me and we had a fight. I didn't know he had a knife. He stabbed me here. (*Points below her shoulder blade, near the heart.*) He punctured my left lung, and I had to be taken to the hospital in a rush. My mother and younger brother begged him to let me go so they could take me to the hospital, but he said, "If you dare take her to the hospital or call the police, something will happen to you. I'll be the one who takes her to the hospital." Of course, my mom was scared, but I told her not to worry, that she should let him. I didn't care who took me—I just knew I needed to be there. So, he took me to the hospital, shamelessly, and said that I was robbed in the street and injured by the robber.

I was taken to intensive care with a tube in me to drain the blood. I was hospitalized for a full month. The doctors said I barely made it. They said I was so lucky.

I couldn't do it anymore. I had to leave. I didn't know how, but I had to. I feared for the lives of those I loved and for my own too. I said to myself, "I will do everything I can to get the money to get away from here, to do something, because I can't take this anymore. The next time, he is going to kill me and my daughter and my mother and my family."

My mother suffered a lot as well. She suffered too much with that. I am her only daughter, among her sons. I am a mother too. I have a daughter too. I can't imagine what it must feel like to witness that happening to your child. No.

I had an older brother who lived in New York. I told him about my situation, and he said I should go to the United States. He told me about all the land crossing routes, but the truth is, I am very fearful. I am a coward, and I said no, I can't do that. I can't cross that way.

So, I made myself presentable and asked for a tourist visa. And thank God I went to the embassy, and well, I was lucky. I was so lucky. Because they gave me and my daughter, who was twelve by then, our visas. God helped me. God heard me. He brought us here.

The first stop was at Immigration, in the airport in Colombia. The officers took a long time with us, asking us many questions. I convinced them that my daughter and I were just going on vacation. I told them I had a job, and my daughter had school, but they wouldn't stop asking questions and treating us like criminals. They asked us if we were smuggling drugs and so on. They treated us horribly, even though we had a visa. It was a very ugly interrogation. I'm sure it still is. They treat you like you're a delinquent, even the children. But we passed. They let us through.

I had never been on a plane before, and I was terrified. We had a stopover in Florida, and I got off the plane feeling like throwing up. I didn't want to know anything more about airplanes. It was a rough flight. (*Laughs.*)

In Florida, we were interrogated again. The rest of the people went through without any problems. They presented their passports and flight tickets, and that was it. But when it was our turn, they stopped us and took us away.

I was carrying a carry-on suitcase with my daughter's toys, books, and notebooks. They opened it, threw everything out, and broke some of it. They took us to another room, and I was so afraid. My daughter was afraid too. I was thinking, "My God, Most Holy, help me. Please help me. What is this? What are they doing? What now? Are they sending us back?"

I was terrified of being sent back to Colombia, to that man, and losing all the money we had spent. I couldn't imagine losing so much money. We had another flight to take, and my daughter knew it was very soon. She said, "Mommy, what's up? Let's go, mommy. We're going to miss our flight."

Luckily, our flight was delayed. Otherwise, we would have missed it, and I don't know what I would have done. Anyway, the officer was not nice. She said she was going to put a red alert on me, and that if I didn't present myself for my flight back, she would put my face in every airport, bus station, and everywhere else until they found me and sent me back to my country.

I was terrified, and because of that, I have never traveled since I arrived in New York nine years ago. I have never left the small radius in which I live and work, because maybe she did put that alert on me. In nine years, I have never gone to another city, a nearby town, or anywhere else. It scares me too much. I'm too afraid to travel, even though I wish I could. I would like to know what's around New York City. I would like to visit Mexico. I have many Mexican coworkers who say it is a beautiful country, and even though I don't eat spicy food, I love tamales. And of course, I would love to be able to visit Colombia. No, not Colombia. But I would like to be able to visit my mom.

She is very calm because we are here and better off. We are safe now. So, my greatest desire, believe me, is to bring her here to me one day. But we are illegal immigrants with no papers, and she is an older woman. I don't know how I could bring her here or how I could see her ever again.

I watched a lot of television in Colombia, and I saw New York in the movies, and it was so beautiful. I remember wondering if I would ever visit that place someday.

And here I was. (*Laughs.*) My brother and his family welcomed me when I arrived, and my first job was as a nanny in their house. The problem was, his wife is a little, well, delicate. (*Laughs.*) We didn't get along very well. My brother wanted her to go to work, or at least help around the house, as he needed her support. However, she didn't want to work, either inside or outside the home. So, they gave me that job: cooking, cleaning, taking care of the children, and so on. I sent almost all the money I made to my mother, but I started to feel more and more like I was stealing money from my brother. After all, his wife was there, in the same apartment as me, and he already had enough debts and financial responsibilities. Having him pay me a salary on top of everything else because his wife refused to work just didn't feel right.

So, I talked to him and told him, "If you want to help me, find me another job." And he did. That's how I entered the world of cooking. I've been working in this restaurant ever since, and it's been wonderful. I'm very grateful for the opportunity because I didn't know anything. They taught me everything, and they were kind and patient. I've learned so much, and I really love what I do. I'm very grateful for that. Most of the people at work speak Spanish, which has been a huge help for me. English is very difficult for me. In this type of business, the only people who speak English are the owners and the customers. But in the kitchen, we speak Spanish.

Living here without speaking English is difficult because you must communicate all the time—with teachers at school, people on the street, in stores, when you get lost and need help, in offices, and so on. There are many people who are kind and helpful and try to teach you the words you're missing. There are many good people. But there are also other people who are rude, who say nasty things or look at you like you're trash, or who just ignore you even if you're asking for help. But over time, you adapt to things. I've tried hard to learn the language, but it's not easy. I've found English classes, but they're all too expensive for me. I can't afford them in terms of money or time. I have medical bills and rent to pay, and my three daughters need a lot of things. We need things at home, and so on. But I'm doing my best to learn.

The father of my first daughter, that man in Colombia, obviously knew right away that we had left, and he threatened me. He told me that he was going to go to Immigration and tell them about me, and he was going to make me come back. And if I wouldn't come back, he was going to do everything he could, everything in his power to either come here or to hurt us in other ways. He then filed a legal complaint against me for having brought his daughter to the United States without his permission. As a result, I had to once again drop the charges from the last complaint I had made against him, from the time he tried to kill me. That was his condition for dropping his charges for infant subtraction.

Even with all charges dropped, he still told me countless things. He said that he was going to take my daughter away from me. He said, "You might be gone, but your mother is still here. Your little brother is still here. If you don't want to come back to me, you will be coming back to a double funeral. Give me the girl and I won't do anything." I said to myself once more, "No more! I'm not going to put up with this anymore."

I still know about him because we have mutual friends, and he is very manipulative and convinces people to send me his messages and tell him about me. Many times, I've paid people, our mutual friends, for their silence! I've had to change my name on social media countless times, and I've changed my phone number even more often. But he still finds me. I don't know how he does it. He sends me messages, he threatens me, and he doesn't stop. I told him, "Do whatever you have to do. If you must come here and do something, then do what you have to do. But I am not going to come back to you. No more." I said, "No more."

I have nothing back in Colombia, nothing at all except for my mother. I wouldn't want to go back for anything, except to see her once more. She is seventy-two years old now, and she is all alone because my younger brother came here too. Years ago, he had an accident and lost three fingers on his right hand. And having a disability in Colombia is a lifelong sentence. They don't let you work, and they don't give you any other opportunities either. No opportunities, no work, and no support. He tried so hard to find a job, and finally, when he couldn't, he came here. He didn't want to be a burden on anyone, and he didn't want to beg in the streets. Shortly after he came, [someone] broke into my mother's house and robbed her. I worry about her every day.

Here I have my eldest daughter, my husband, and the twin girls we have together. My husband is Colombian too, and he also works in the kitchen. The story is very funny because we found each other here in New York. I met him almost a year after arriving in the United States, but we had known each other in Colombia when we were young, but only by sight. It wasn't until we found each other here that we talked for the first time. We would have never imagined back then that we would be together in a relationship, so far away. (*Laughs.*)

He is, in a way, my soulmate. He is a very good person. He has his issues, oh my God he does. (*Laughs.*) But we've managed to move our family forward. He loves my daughter like his own. And she, my eldest, has helped me a lot. And so has he.

My daughters are very intelligent. One of the twins plays the saxophone. I see her so small, so short, so tiny, and playing such a big instrument. I wonder how she does that. How is that possible? They do very well in school. It's impressive. I am proud of them. And happy for my eldest daughter. If she had to witness all the horrors, then she was also to witness the success.

I'm very grateful to this country because it has given me a lot of things and I've been able to progress. This is a beautiful country, and this is a beautiful city. But even though there are so many people, it can be a lonely place. This is because people here see things differently. Family is very important to humans, and it is something that is essential. But it doesn't seem to be the same way here. This city can give you economic stability, but it cannot give you emotional stability.

The other thing I find strange here and I have a hard time adapting to is that, in my country, you eat breakfast, have a big meal in the middle of the day, and then have dinner. But here, you sometimes have breakfast, never lunch, and then have dinner. Isn't that funny? I've come to learn that you only eat twice a day here, if you have the time! Because that's the problem, you have so much to do, you forget to eat. For me, the only way I eat well is when I'm at home. Because I like to eat sitting down, and I like to take my time, to really nourish myself and to smell and appreciate the food. I can't rush it. I can't have a bite of this and a bite of that while working. What helps are soups. (*Laughs.*)

My country has the most delicious soups. Colombian soups are the best of the best, and there is a special soup called *ajiaco* that I absolutely adore. *Ajiaco* is a dish from Bogotá, and it is based on three types of potatoes: creole potato, yellow potato, and either *arracacha* or *sabanera* potato. It comes with chicken and corn on the cob, and it is served with cream and capers on top. It is so rich and delicious. I love it!

There is another dish called *changua*. It is like a breakfast dish, a mixture of water, milk, toasted bread, butter, salt, eggs, cilantro, and onion. You mix them together and then cook them. The eggs are semi-hard. For us, it is a delight. I have made it at work here, and well . . . Some of my coworkers liked it, others didn't, and some wouldn't even try it because they said that the mixture of milk and salt doesn't seem too appetizing to them. (*Laughs.*) I crave a lot of food from where I come from, like corn *arepas* filled with cheese, and hot chocolate with cheese cubes. Oh my God, I'm dying! They are so delicious!

I would like to set up my own food business serving delicious Colombian food or food from various Latin American countries. That is my dream. I want to make something for myself, and most of all, I want to be able to leave something to my daughters because I don't have anything. I don't know if I will achieve this dream because the economic situation is difficult, everything here is very expensive, and on top of that, I have horribly bad teeth.

I'm going through a very long and difficult dental treatment. About four years ago, I had surgery to remove two front teeth. Bone was also removed, so the entire front portion of my mouth is being repaired. Eight teeth need to be restored, fixed, or replaced. It's very difficult and ugly, especially for a woman—it's just bad for the self-esteem. But most of all, it's expensive. I had to pay $600 today, and I'll have to pay another $900 on Monday. A few days ago, I paid $2,000, and each visit costs at least $150. It never seems to end. It's horrible because I don't always have that much money. Twice, the temporaries have fallen out and I've had to get new ones. To be honest, it's been quite tough. But one day, I'll be finished. And then I can start saving up for my dream again: my own restaurant. In my country, I sold empanadas, *arepas*, and lunches on the streets. I did whatever it took to move forward, because life is up to you.

In my life, things are beautiful. But inside my head, it is very, very dark. I am currently going to a psychologist because I am suffering from anxiety and depression. All the bad things I went through in Colombia have come back to haunt me inside my head and inside my heart. There are days when I can't sleep or rest well. I was diagnosed with lupus more than a year ago, and it is attacking my bones. I have pain in my back, neck, elbows, hands, and legs. The pain can get very strong, and sometimes it mixes together with the pain that lives in my heart, the pain of the things I've lived through.

The doctor who treats me for lupus gives me a lot of medications, but many of them keep me awake at night. Often, as I lie there in bed in the dark, my mind wanders and remembers, and I have panic attacks. It feels like something is going to happen. I get up from bed with that feeling and wonder, "Is my mother okay in Colombia? Has that man found me here? Is he breaking in?" I don't know how to describe it, but it's a horrible feeling. It comes with a feeling of emptiness in my stomach, like a black hole, a void. And at the same time, it's like too much—too much of everything I've been through in Colombia with him, with my child's father, and everything my stepfather did to me. All of that is like a knot in my chest, like a knot in my soul, and sometimes it makes me feel bad, very bad. Sometimes I don't want to . . . be anymore. There are days when I don't . . . when I feel like I can't go on. Because there are a lot of things. There were many years of abuse, many years of being emptied.

And the fear is still there. If someday I could suddenly have papers or some legal status and I could travel to Colombia to visit my mother, what if he gets me then? People tell me that he never stopped believing that someday I will be "his" again, that we would get back together, and in spite of so many years, he has never gotten married. He is obsessed. What if he finds a way to get me back legally? He has sued me, he has denounced me to the authorities, and he said he would come.

My husband and daughters try to keep me calm, and I focus a lot on my work, which helps a lot. I am on my fourth session of therapy, and it has helped me to be able to get things off my chest. Because after keeping things secret for so long, you get a lump in your throat and start to believe that no one will care to listen. And there are indeed many people who don't care, but there are also people who do. And little by little, I can rest from all the pain and fear that I have inside.

I try to heal myself because I think it is the best thing I can do for my daughters. If I want them to have a different life than mine, I have to make a lot of effort to make sure they don't live the same life. For example, I talk to my daughters a lot about abuse. I make it very clear that no one, absolutely no one, can touch them, treat them badly, or belittle them. Absolutely no one. If their father one day makes them do things that don't feel right, they always have to talk about it. They must say something. Nobody can disrespect them, nobody.

There is nothing I wouldn't do for my daughters. I would die for them but also I am willing to live for them in a way that serves them, that helps them. We talk a lot—I ask them every day how they are doing. I ask them about their day, and they tell me what they ate, what they played, what they did. We talk about everything; they are my everything. (*Smiles.*)

ÁNGEL

I'm from Tehuacán, [Mexico,] a town an hour and a half away from Puebla City. We were a big family, with five boys and three girls. It was crazy, but we got along and helped each other. My mom took care of the house and us, while my dad worked as a truck driver. There was a big family-owned farm in our town. They produced crops, chickens, cooking oil, and all kinds of things, and almost everyone worked for them, including my dad. He drove their eggs to many cities in the country—to Acapulco, Veracruz, or Tuxtla [Gutierrez]. Back then, there were not many highways, so trips took longer, and he often was gone for three or four days.

At home, we were all involved in daily life and work. At some point we opened a grocery store in our house, a small neighborhood store, to generate some extra income, and we all helped run it. On the weekends, we would go to the market to buy the products we needed for the store, and I was in charge of getting the bread. I would go to the bakery and come back with a big basket of bread to sell.

My mom did so many things. She made everything we needed in terms of clothing, from school uniforms to suits or dresses for special occasions. She had a sewing machine and everything. She also took care of the finances. Every Saturday, our dad would give her his paycheck. She managed the whole family.

My dad didn't have much education, maybe first or second grade. He came from a big family and started working very young. My mom is more educated; I think she completed elementary school. Her family owned a bakery, lands, sheep, cows, and they had a big store in town.

There was a rule in our family that when you were fourteen or fifteen and didn't want to continue going to school, you had to start working. So, some of my brothers started working at a young age—at thirteen or fourteen—but I kept going. I always knew that education was the only way to move forward. We saw poverty around us, people who had less than us, and I think that taught all of us that it is very important to keep doing what we are doing and to get better at it.

When I was sixteen years old, I went to Mexico City. I wanted to attend UNAM, the University of Mexico, and my idea was to get into their system, complete my high school diploma in one of their schools, and that way I would save time and start university earlier, as if I had applied just after completing regular high school in my hometown. Also, I wanted to be there already, have a head start, and get the experience of a bigger city.

I was in Mexico City for almost two years and [was] almost done with my high school when my dad lost his job. That was especially bad because in Mexico, if you are older than forty-five, it's very hard to find a new job. So, my family was in trouble—we needed to do something.

Of course, we knew of people who went to the United States. People from my mother's town were among the first to come to New York back then, and we had cousins who were already living here. So, when my father lost his job, my oldest brother was supposed to come here. But he didn't make it. He got killed because of a bad friendship with a neighbor. He was stabbed to death in a house in Tehuacán before he could leave.

So instead of him, my other older brother went to New York. Meanwhile, I finished high school, left Mexico City, and returned to my hometown. My family was struggling in those days, trying to find a way to make it. Then, a year after he left, my brother came back. It was never my plan to leave Mexico, but he had saved enough money to get me and my sixteen-year-old brother to New York. So we took the opportunity and went.

We flew from Mexico City to Tijuana, where we met a coyote. We arrived at his house in the evening, and in the middle of the night, he said, "Let's go," and we crossed the border. Some people went straight, but he told us to go around, so we walked a big arc, crossing mountains and highways, and around five in the morning, we were on the other side. From there, they took us in a car to San Diego, where we waited a couple of days for more people to join us. Then they put us on a plane to New York.

I arrived here in 1990. I was nineteen years old and started working in a grocery store in the Bronx for a couple of days until I got a job as a dishwasher in an Italian restaurant in the Upper East Side. Later, they needed a salad person, so I was trained for a couple of days and started making salads. I also went to school to learn English. I knew the basics from high school, but I needed more. So I changed jobs, made a little bit more money, and with whatever extra I made, I would pay for my school.

Somehow, I ended up in charge of the kitchen at a tiny café on 84th and Madison. They had a little electric burner for making pastas. I used to read a lot to learn more things, and with the knowledge gained from reading and the experience I already had, I was able to run that little kitchen. It was there that I met my first wife, an American Jew—she was the manager.

After finishing English school, I went to culinary school. I wanted to work in a big restaurant, build a strong résumé, and just keep going. That was always my thinking: to get better and keep going. So, I enrolled in Peter Kump's New York Cooking School, which is now the Institute of Culinary Education, the ICE. I was working full-time while attending the courses, which was hard, but having a solid understanding of cooking techniques gave me a great deal of confidence.

Because I was married, I was able to get my green card, and therefore I could travel. My wife and I did backpacking in Europe. We went to Spain, France, Italy, and Greece. It was fantastic, mind-opening, and just . . . wow. I never thought I would be able to do this, but there I was, a kid from Tehuacán, seeing all these places, people, and things. Never forget where you are coming from, never—it makes you want more. You want to do better, provide more, see and know more, and explore new things.

When I came back from Europe, I did my internship at Jean-Georges, and when he opened the Mercer Kitchen, I worked there for almost two years. After that, I went to Guastavino's, located under the Queensboro

Bridge, for about a year. Then, I went to Connecticut and worked there for six months, commuting every day.

During that time, my wife and I separated after six years. It was a difficult period for me. Back then I was drinking, and I started drinking more. I went back to Mexico as often as I could, stayed at my parents' house, and continued drinking. I would work in the States for six months, save some money, quit my job, go home for two months, come back, and do the same thing over again. Not a good time. At some point I guess I was done with the breakup. I stabilized myself again and started to work in new places. And that's when I came to the Bowery Group, to Cookshop, in 2005.

To be honest, on my first day, I thought I would just last a year here. (*Laughs.*) When I saw you that day, I was wondering, "What is that man doing?" At Guastavino's, there was a guy who butchered and did other tasks, acting as if he was the owner, but he wasn't. So, when I saw you butchering on my first day and then changing for the service, putting on your jacket and going for the pass, I thought, "Ah, okay, he is one of those." However, it wasn't until I went downstairs and saw your picture in that *New York Times* review that I realized you *were* the owner! (*Laughs.*)

Two years later, in 2007, I met my second wife. She is a friend of my sister. In 2008, our son was born, and in 2014, our daughter. I worked at Cookshop for ten years until we opened Rosie's in 2015. That was an interesting transition. I could use all the knowledge, exposure to techniques, and management experience I had gained over the years. Here is the thing: when you prepare yourself for more, more will happen. I tell the guys in the kitchen that when I need help with something, they shouldn't see it as extra work. Instead, they should view it as an opportunity to learn something new. Later, they will know how to do it, and when they work with someone else and that person sees how organized and skilled they are, they will end up in a better position.

My son is fifteen now, and he works hard. He wants to do big things. Since he was little, his dream has been to go to Harvard. He wants to be a doctor one day, working in the field of medicine. Currently he attends Phillips Exeter Academy in New Hampshire, one of the best private schools in the United States. It has always been important to me that my kids know where they come from, and I'm happy to see that my son is now very into Mexico. He wears a Mexico cap and wants to take a Mexican flag to school and put it in his window. He knows his heritage and is proud of it. And he knows, when we go home to Mexico, he has to be careful.

I have never regretted leaving Mexico. If I had stayed, we wouldn't have what we have now, and I would be in a difficult situation. Over there it's very hard, and even if you save money here and go back with the intention of building something up, it's unlikely that you will achieve your goals. Most people end up having to come back here.

Our city is very big now. When we were kids the neighborhood we lived in was countryside, with only a few other houses and open spaces. There was a small river where my mother used to wash clothes, and when there were heavy rains, it would overflow and clean the streets a bit. We loved that river. We used to build dams with rocks and create a pool to swim. But then the clothing factories started to appear, and the water got dirty.

Now it's very bad. The water smells of the chemicals the factories dump in there. They are clothing factories mostly, and the chemicals they use to dye and wash the clothes all go into the river. Also, there is not much water anymore. Even when it rains, the river never overflows. When the factories came, they needed people, many people came, and the town grew bigger and bigger. Then the factories declined. Most of them are still there but not as strong as before. Many people lost their jobs.

When you go to Tehuacán and see how people live, it's sad, especially after COVID. Many people who were in an okay situation lost everything. A few months ago, my sister and I went to a store to get some ice cream, and a man helped us open the car door. When we returned to the car, he held the door open for us again. My sister told me that he used to work as a server at a restaurant she often went to. He has a wife and kids, but due to COVID, he lost his job. There are many stories like that. My son sees kids selling candies on the streets and is aware of his advantages. He wants to help and do something. The government is not doing anything. The Mexican president claims that Mexico is safer than the United States, but who is supposed to believe that?

When we were kids, we used to walk to the river, go for a swim, and on the way back we would stop at one of the *pulquerias*. That's where they sell *escotes*, snails. We loved them, but going there to get them was crazy because those *pulquerias* were seedy bars and not really places for kids. (*Laughs.*) But that's something I still try to do when I go home: eat snails, *barbacoa*, roasted chicken, *huaraches*, and *tacos arabes*.

My mom is an excellent cook. Raising a family with so many kids and trying to make something different and seasonal every day on a tight budget was quite a challenge. When I'm cooking, I have the smells of her cooking in my memory. I remember how the house smelled every time my mother cooked something. It could be as simple as fried eggs or black beans, but there was a specific smell that you recognize. And when I'm cooking here in New York, at our restaurant, like when we make the mole, and I get that smell, I know I'm doing it right.

One of my favorite dishes my mother makes is *jaibas en chilpachole*. It's a lot of work because you have to break the shell of the crab, and it's also a lot of work to eat it, but it's worth it. She makes it spicy with lots of chipotle, which makes you sweat and your nose run, and you enjoy it! (*Laughs.*)

Back then, there was this tiny town called Coapan outside of Tehuacán where we used to go to the market every Saturday. I loved going to the market with my mother. I helped her, and she would get me a snack like a taco with scrambled potato, rice, and egg, all wrapped in a big tortilla, or some *tacos de barbacoa*. In Coapan, they sold the most delicious *barbacoa*. There were these tiny food stands; they had the base already prepared—it's all about the base, the stock—and they just put the meat in.

Outside the market, there is still the old lady who sells *tacos de canasta*. She has a big basket full of steamed tortillas filled with mole sauce, and maybe some sesame seeds and lettuce, that's all she sells, and it's fantastic.

Going to the San Lorenzo market is one of the things I do every time I go home, just to see the *chicharron*, the mole, all the stands with their fruits and vegetables, all fresh from the area. And then the section where they sell corn and *huitlacoche*, the real one, fresh! All of that—the flavors, the smells, the colors—it's just a good experience. That's what I do: I fly home, wake up at seven in the morning on a Saturday, and go to the market.

DIEGO

I am from Ecuador, from a small town near Azogues. My mother only went to school for two years. She got married at the age of fifteen, and my father was eighteen. They married, and a year later I was born, their first child. I have three brothers and one sister.

My childhood wasn't easy, but it was good. Nowadays, kids have so many choices and things to play with; we simply played soccer in the streets and had fun. I wasn't aware of my family's poverty until I was about ten years old. That's when I realized that we didn't have a proper house. Our home was just a hut with a kitchen on one end and a single bed behind a partition where we all slept. After I became aware of our poverty, I thought about it a lot.

My mother sold fruits at the plaza in town, and my father . . . Well, he had gone to the United States when I was four years old. He was the first person from his town to do so, and maybe that's why it was so hard for him. He had no family there, no friends. The first time he went, he sent money, but when he returned to Ecuador, he drank for six months and then went back to New York. However, that second time he didn't send money; he just drank and drank and returned as a broken man. He had worked as a busser and lived with eighteen other guys in a three-room apartment in Queens. Fifteen years later, when I came to the United States, I stayed in that same apartment. It took me two trips to get here. I almost didn't make it.

I stopped going to school when I was ten. It had to do with realizing our poverty and also because my school was two hours away from home. I had to walk that distance every day—two hours to get there and two hours back. Sometimes it was raining, other times it was very sunny. It just didn't make sense anymore, and we needed money. My father wasn't helping; he was drinking. We didn't have much land to grow things—just a hut with a small patch where we raised chickens, rabbits, and *cuy* [guinea pigs]. So, I told my mother that from then on, I would work.

And I did. When I was eleven years old, I started working for my aunt. She seemed rich to me because she had a truck. She and my uncle would drive five hours to the coast to buy fruits, flowers, and sugar and then sell them in town. I helped them with that. Every time my aunt took me on one of their trips, I watched my uncle drive. I saw how he used the gears and so on. Then one of my uncles bought a car and parked it in front of our house. Sometimes, when my mother went to the plaza to sell fruits, I took the key and taught myself how to drive. (*Laughs.*) That's why I knew how to drive when I was twelve years old. Two years later, that skill came in handy.

There was this guy who sometimes drove the truck for my aunt, and occasionally I went with him to help. On that day though, he was drunk—very drunk. I had the money for the fruits, knew the route, and knew how to drive. So, I went on my own. I drove to the coast, bought mandarins, melons, and green plantains, and then drove back. My mother didn't like it. I didn't have a driver's license—what if the police caught me? But in my country, you could just pay the police, and they would let you be. So, I started to drive to the coast on my own.

Back then, the bananas they exported to other countries, the ones they thought were not great, they tossed them out at the side of the road. Most were still good; there was nothing wrong with them. They were just too small or too big for export, but they were just tossed out, and they were for free. So, I filled up the truck with the bananas, brought them back home, and waited a couple of days for them to change color from green to yellow, and then I started to sell them. I made 1,500 sucres per trip. That was a lot of money back then. Soon I was making two or three trips a week, just by myself. It took five hours to go there and five hours to come back, sometimes longer on the way back because a full truck is slower.

This went on for years; that's how I made money. I even managed to buy myself my own old truck. Sometimes I went to another town, which took nine hours to get there and nine to eleven hours back, all in one day. To stay awake, I mixed two liters of cola with black coffee, ate candy, and smoked cigarettes. My last trip was two days before I tried to come to the United States for the first time; I was nineteen then.

That week, it rained and rained and rained. I went to the coast, got my bananas, and went back. But my truck got stuck in the mud. I could save and sell the bananas, but my truck was stuck there for three days. When the rain finally stopped, I went to retrieve it, but it was broken. Something underneath was so badly damaged that it didn't make sense to fix it.

So, I said to my mother, "I've tried to make it here, but I don't think it's going to be possible. I'm going to go to the United States." And my mom, she was crying, crying, crying. Because I was their support. My father had been back for a long time, but he was drinking, only drinking. He was a good man when he wasn't drinking, but when he was drunk, he forgot his family. He forgot everything.

[In] my home, the land is small hills and there is no jungle. People farm, they have some animals, but getting by is difficult. I don't know how the older people did it. My grandfather had two wives and eleven children with each wife, twenty-two children in total, and I don't know how he did it. He passed away four years ago, and I never asked him.

I borrowed money from a coyote to get me here. He charged me $8,000. I was supposed to give him $3,500 in Ecuador and the rest when I was in the US. So, I went for the first time in my life to Quito, the capital, which was eight hours away. From there, I flew to Panama; I had never flown before. In Panama, I took a bus. Then, we walked for three nights to get to Costa Rica. During the day, we hid in the jungle. There were twenty-two people in total, with three women and the rest being men.

In Costa Rica, there was a big truck with a trailer that was filled with cow skins. They had made two small spaces in between these stacks of cow hides with a small hole on top, and they put eleven of us in each section. Then they closed the trailer, and the truck drove for nine hours through Costa Rica to Nicaragua. It was so hot. There was no air inside, and the skins were stinky.

About twenty minutes before the truck stopped, some stacks of skins fell and crashed into the other section where the other group was. People were screaming and crying, "Help! Help!" We tried to get through to them and remove the skins, but there were so many, and they were heavy. Somehow, we managed to make it, and nobody died. Then the truck stopped. They opened the doors, and it was night, surrounded by jungle. They said, "Go in there and hide."

Sometime later, someone came and said, "OK, let's walk." We walked for six hours until we reached a house where we stayed for four days. This was in Nicaragua. Then they came with a windowless van to take us to another town. The van didn't have any seats, so they told us to sit with our legs open, close together, one person after the other, like stacked. We sat on the floor in four lines and drove for an hour. Then the van stopped, and we heard there was a control, some checkpoint, so we didn't make a sound.

We started driving again, but the driver must have gotten nervous. I don't know how he did it, but he hit one of the cops with the van's side mirror. The cops stopped us again, and five minutes later we were surrounded by a thousand police officers. If it hadn't been for the driver's mistake, we would have passed, but now we all went to jail.

They put us in a cell, all twenty-two of us together. There were holes in the wall up high; that's where the air came in. We must have been close to the jungle because we could sometimes see big frogs and snakes, but they never came inside. We stayed there for twenty-two days. Then they informed us that if we could pay for our ticket, we could fly back to Ecuador the next day. Otherwise, we would have to wait for two more weeks. I had some money hidden and spent it all.

I was always skinny, but when I came back home, I was just skin and bones. The guy I had paid, the coyote, said he would send another group the following week and I could try again, but I couldn't. I was too weak. So, my brother Luis,* who is four years younger than me, went instead. And he made it on his first attempt.

---

* See Luis's story on page 197.

Five months later, he called me, crying, "I need you here, I'm so alone." He was in Queens, in that apartment, with my uncles, but he didn't know them. He had never seen them before. "I have nobody here. You have to come." I had taken care of him since he was a baby, so I said, "OK."

This time, the coyote, another guy, wanted $12,000, and $5,000 was needed upfront. So, I borrowed more money, despite already owing so much. I paid him, and within a week, he disappeared with the $5,000. When I found another person to help me, he charged $9,000 just to start. I knew I had to make it this time. I couldn't afford to fail again.

Again, I traveled to Quito and took a flight to Panama, but then I took a plane to Mexico, to Guadalajara. There, I waited for five days. Then, I flew to Toluca, near Mexico City, and spent two days waiting. Finally, I took a flight to Los Angeles, all without proper documents. The coyotes helped me arrange the tickets.

At customs, the guy didn't ask me for ID or anything. He just asked me for my name. I think the coyotes paid him and knew where he would be, because they told me exactly when and where to go. They said to me, "They're going to ask you for your name. You say your name, and then you say my name. Then you're free. Keep going. Don't look back. Just pass." I did that. Then I took a bus from LA to New York City. I arrived here on July 22nd in 1999.

I arrived at Grand Central, finally. It had taken me eighteen days to get to New York. I took the 7 train to Queens, where my brother Luis was living in the same apartment our father had stayed in fifteen years ago. Three days later, I got my first job as a dishwasher in an Italian restaurant. On my second day of work, I had to go to the basement with a big pot to get sauce, and I don't know how it happened, but I slipped and fell down the stairs.

I got up and checked myself, but nothing was broken, so I got the sauce, brought it back to the chef (who happened to be an Ecuadorian guy), and continued washing dishes. While working, I felt something on my head, and when I looked at my fingers, there was blood. I informed the chef about what had happened, but he didn't say much, so I just kept on working. After finishing my shift, I went back home, took a shower, and noticed that my back was turning purple, with some parts of the skin scraped off. I also had back pain and a headache. My brother Luis said, "And you're still working after that? Are you crazy?" And I was like, "Yeah." (*Laughs.*)

But you know, that was my first job. They paid me $220, and I was so excited. However, in the end, I never worked the eight hours they had told me I would. Instead, I worked twelve or fourteen hours without any extra pay. So, I decided to leave and found a job at the same restaurant where my brother worked. They offered me $340, and I accepted. I worked there for almost three years.

For our trips and attempts to cross, my brother and I owed a total of $25,000, and the interest was 5 percent. So, for a year and a half, almost everything we were making, all the money, we were sending away to pay off that debt. After we were done, we bought ourselves new clothes. Before that, we never bought anything, not even a bottle of water. Now we could buy shoes and soda; now we were free.

I met my wife when I tried to bring my sister here, sixteen years ago. She and a friend—my future wife—had bought visas from a woman in Ecuador, not knowing that the visas were fake. They flew from Ecuador to Miami, where they got caught and put in jail for two months. During that time, the parents of my future wife often called me to ask if I knew anything new about her because she was with my sister. So, we started talking, my future wife and me.

When she was back in Ecuador, she told me that it had been her third try to come to the US. She didn't want to try it again, but she was owing some people so much money by then for all the failed attempts that she didn't have a choice. My sister decided to stay in Ecuador. She said, "That's it. I've been in jail for two months, and I don't want to be there again."

Finally, my future wife made it to New York. She was here for two days before she called me. "Hi, it's me, Sara," she said. "I'm here." She was living three blocks away. I asked her if I could invite her to a coffee. So, we met, and she told me the story of her crossing, and we started talking and never really stopped. (*Laughs.*) At that time, I was already working at Cookshop and at Uptown on 84th and Broadway. I always had two jobs.

Now Sara, my wife, is the mother of my kids. We have been living together for fifteen years. My grandmother always said, "You don't have to look for love—it will come to you." And so it was. We have two children. Our son is fourteen years old; our daughter is twelve. And that's it, no more kids! (*Laughs.*) I'm so proud. Sara is a wonderful mother and partner. She has also changed my life because, you know, when you're all by yourself, you don't think so much about what you're doing and if it's good for you. But when you find someone you love, you start to think differently because you are not alone anymore.

VLAD

My name is Vladislav, but most people here call me Vlad. I am from Bosnia and Herzegovina, which was still Yugoslavia when I was born in 1982. Back then, there were six republics: Slovenia, Croatia, Bosnia and Herzegovina, Serbia, Montenegro, and Macedonia. In school, when I was a kid before the war, we spoke Serbo-Croatian. That was the official language of Yugoslavia, and it was written in both the Latin and Cyrillic alphabets. We learned and used them both—one week Latin, one week Cyrillic. Most of my childhood I spent in Sarajevo, the capital of Bosnia.

My life from kindergarten to elementary school was good. I had a bicycle and played soccer on the street, but many things were different. Yugoslavia was a Communist country, very protected from the outside. And it was a peaceful country. There was almost no crime, or perhaps they just didn't tell us—but for example, kids went to school on their own. Every morning, I locked our apartment and walked to school with all the other kids in my neighborhood. That's how safe it was. Now it has changed. Now it's like everywhere else.

My mom was a cook in a furniture factory; she made food for three hundred workers in the company's canteen, where you paid with vouchers. At the beginning of each month, you would receive a couple of dozens of these papers along with your paycheck, and you used them to pay for your food. You could even bring your family or trade these vouchers for other things.

My father was a carpenter who worked for the same company until after the 1984 Winter Olympics, when he got a new job as a maintenance supervisor at a complex of hotels and sports facilities that had been built for the Games.

We were neither rich nor poor. We were working class, like most people. Products from the West—like matchbox cars, transformer figures, or Coca-Cola—were hard to get or very expensive. But Yugoslavia produced its own versions of many Western products. Instead of Nutella, we had something similar called Kinder Lada, and the alternative for Coca-Cola was called Kokta. The Yugoslavian equivalent of the Fiat 500 was the Zastava 750, and for many years, a Yugoslavian version of the Volkswagen Golf was produced in Sarajevo. The country, despite being a Communist nation, was pretty open and for a time, economically very strong.

Parents were very strict, though, not just mine. You had to listen to them. Discipline was important, and if you went to someone's house, you knew how to behave. You would not touch anything—[you would] sit down and be quiet. You would never ask for anything, but if they offered you something, you could say yes. That strictness was everywhere: in kindergarten, school, and the family. We had huge respect for our teachers and our neighbors, especially our neighbors, because they knew your mom, and if they complained about you, Mom would beat you. That was very normal.

In my family, we never talked about politics or religion. Whenever my parents watched the news, I had to go to my room. The news was very important for them, but I think they wanted to protect me from these things. I am Orthodox, Serbian Christian Orthodox, but I didn't know that until the war began. In Communism, there is no religion. It is not taught—you do not go to church, and if you believe in it, you hide it. We did not celebrate Christmas, Easter, or any other religious festivities, and I didn't know if people were Muslim, Evangelical, Orthodox, or Catholic Christian. Grown-ups could tell by people's names, [which] were often chosen according to their religious background, but I had no clue until the war began.

I was still in elementary school when things started to change. Suddenly, there were new kids because the republics of Slovenia and Croatia had declared independence. The Yugoslav People's Army went to the borders, fighting began, and we got those new kids in school. That was when I first heard about what would then become the war.

Before that, the economy had gotten bad. Many people lost their jobs, and my parents no longer got paid. Instead, they received *bonovi*, special vouchers from the company that could be used to purchase food from stores. But the shelves were empty, black markets were beginning to spring up everywhere, it was all falling apart. When the war started, I was ten years old. I remember everything. It's like putting together a mosaic.

The war started on April 6, 1992. From one day to the next, everything changed. There were shootings in Sarajevo, the roads were blocked, you couldn't leave the city. My mother, my sister, and I were in our apartment without my father, who had been sent to the Olympic hotel complex to close everything down in case something happened. When the shootings started, we lost contact with him.

Sarajevo used to be a multiethnic city. Before the Bosnian War, the population was maybe 50 percent Muslim, 30 percent Orthodox Christian/Serbian, and 10 percent Catholic/Croatian. But now the war led to a rise in nationalism among the different ethnic groups, and many people began to support independence for their own ethnic group. That's basically what the war was about, which now happened all around us in the city.

It was before the bombings; there were just shootings, but it was very scary. We knew we had to leave somehow because it started with the Green Berets, the Bosnian Muslim paramilitary units. They were checking apartments, especially those of Serbs, looking for guns and other things. They hadn't knocked on our door yet, but we were in a panic because we had just seen how they took our neighbors, who were also Serbian. We left the next day.

We wanted to go to my aunt who lived in a suburb of Sarajevo, in the Serbian part. But there were barricades everywhere, and we heard the shootings. It was so scary. I remember us crossing a few streets and going to a bus stop or something; then a man picked us up in a car and drove us a few miles. I remember barricades with soldiers, but they were Serbian soldiers, not Yugoslav soldiers. I think there were already four different armies by then: the Bosnian, the Croatian, the Serbs, and the Yugoslav. I didn't know who the good guys were. I just saw all these guns and heard the shootings, and I was scared.

We made it to my aunt's house, my father's sister. Shortly afterwards, my father managed to call my mother there and told her to go back to our apartment and get all our important papers—birth certificates, passports, and so on. She hadn't taken them before, and only got the money, which was worthless. So, my mother left, which was extremely dangerous, but she didn't know that they were shooting at civilians by now. She made it back to the apartment, spent the night there, and the next day she tried to walk back to the Serbian side. Again, she was lucky, and no one shot at her. But because of the fighting, she didn't get very far. Luckily, she found refuge in a Yugoslav/Serbian army base, where she stayed almost the whole summer. She was free to go but couldn't cross; she was stuck.

The first few weeks, we didn't know anything. She just hadn't come back, and we couldn't call my dad; we were terrified, worried sick—it was horrible. We were with my aunt until finally we got the news that she was okay and safe. But we still didn't know anything about our father.

He was at the Olympic hotel complex, basically trapped there with two other men: another Serb and a Muslim. By that time, the hotel complex was in Muslim territory. One day, the Muslim told my father and the other man, "You should go. They will come and take over the hotel tomorrow. It's not safe for you anymore." So, they left that same evening, crossing the lines by night, over the mountains and through the woods to the Serbian side, where they were immediately given guns. By then, it was like that. There were basically no male civilians anymore. Every man between eighteen and sixty was part of some army, whatever army there was where he was. Every man had a rifle or some kind of gun, even if he didn't have a uniform. But now, at least, my dad was on our side, and every now and then he came to visit us at my aunt's for one or two days.

We were so lucky to be at my aunt's house, because we were on the Serbian side and by then the Serbs were dominant. We heard the fighting, the shootings, the bombings; we saw the news on the few channels that were left, but it was all strangely far from us. We were playing in the garden behind the house while people were getting killed in the city. We survived on the food that the United Nations brought in to help; we lived on canned goods, toasted bread, and milk powder. And then, on December 14, 1995, after almost four years, the war ended.

The United States and Western Europe finally managed to end the madness with the Dayton Agreement. The moment it was signed, the fighting stopped, just like that. Of course we celebrated, but only for a few days, until we realized what had been signed: the Serbs had to leave Sarajevo. We had to leave our apartment, my aunt and uncle had to leave their house, all the Serbs had to go. I think we had about a month.

People went wherever they knew someone who could help them. We went to Modriča, a city in the north of the country where my mother's family lived. Luckily, one of my uncles had lived in Germany since the 1970s and sent us money, so we could pay for a truck to transport most of our belongings, and that's how we moved north and started over. For me this meant new school, new life, new everything.

It wasn't easy. During the war, people were praying for the fighting and killing to stop, and when it finally ended, they realized that they had destroyed everything. There was nothing left. That took a big toll on my parents' generation. We teenagers, well . . . At that age, you just want to hang out with your friends, listen to music, buy new clothes, have a normal life, but all of that was impossible. It was all gone. The first five years after the war were difficult, especially for our parents. They had to rebuild everything. And even after that, there was still all that hate and trauma.

I always had the idea of leaving, even before the war, because I had family living in other countries: uncles and aunts in Germany, Switzerland, and Austria. Like many Yugoslavs, they left in the 1960s or 1970s to work and live abroad. It was a beautiful time, because people didn't need visas to go anywhere, and countries like Germany needed workers. And when I saw my cousins, when they came to visit, they were doing well. They had better clothes, they seemed to know more and were generally different than us. I always thought I would go to Germany one day. Even though most of the culture of my youth came from the USA—I grew up on MTV, I loved George Michael, Iggy Pop, Billy Idol, Michael Jackson, and Madonna—for us, Germany seemed reachable. It was in the West. The USA and a city like New York—well, that was Mars to us, a different planet.

I left when I was still in college. There was this program called Work and Travel, which allowed you to go anywhere. I chose the USA. I had a working visa for six months and got my first job at the Boston Culinary Group in Massachusetts. I worked in the kitchen. Before that, I had no connection with kitchens and cooking. Now I was in Cape Cod preparing sandwiches and salads for the little ferries, the tourist boats that crossed between Cape Cod and all those fancy islands. I started at four o'clock in the morning and worked and worked, and still, the money wasn't enough.

So, I went to New York with $1,200. My English was bad, not even enough for basic conversation. With that, I could have worked in construction, maybe in a moving company, or in the kitchen. I stayed with the kitchen, almost. My first job I found in Brooklyn at Aqualis Grill as a busser. The owner recognized that I was working hard, so after a few months, he offered me the opportunity to become a chef-server at lunch. And that's how my career as a server started.

I was in my early twenties, full of energy. Sometimes, when I had a little bit of money, two or three thousand dollars, which is nothing really, I wanted to go back home, buy new clothes, invite my friends to restaurants, but I wasn't homesick. I was fine where I was, even though I was separated from my parents and everything I ever knew. I don't know—I just always felt like I was running from something. The war is always behind you, the memories of the bad things that happened. You cannot delete them. And in these societies, in those Balkan countries, you don't get a lot of support. Whoever you are, you depend on yourself. Maybe that toughened me up, that and the war and what came after. Maybe that made me stronger.

I needed years and years to become a New Yorker. I was always shy and not comfortable in my skin. Where I come from, we are all the same. We look the same, talk the same, and basically speak the same language, even though we pretend we don't. But here in New York, you won't find anyone to tell your problems to if you can't express yourself. There are not many Serbians here either. And if you find one, he becomes everything for you: your brother, your friend, your father—just because you speak the same language. And you are closer to him than to anyone else, even though he might not be good for you. You trust him just because you come from the same country. I found out that this can be a mistake.

How did I become a star waiter? (*Laughs.*) Well, it's nice that you think so, but I don't know! After my first job as a server, I worked in many different restaurants, always leaving and looking for a new one. I always felt like I didn't belong there. Something always didn't feel right. For example, I always thought that somebody yelling at me meant they didn't like me, but it's very normal in a restaurant. (*Laughs.*) Still, I just didn't want to be anywhere where I wasn't respected. And then I found my place.

When I serve people, I want to show the best of myself. It starts with self-respect. If you don't respect yourself, you can't present yourself or the restaurant well. Also, where I come from, in the Balkan countries, hospitality is a huge thing. We love to bring people into our homes, cook for them, and give them the best we have. It might have a little bit to do with personality too. And of course, you learn a lot; experience is key. Also, experience helped me develop a passion for this industry. Passion and experience lead to success. I think that's the formula. And of course, there is nothing more motivating than realizing that your work is appreciated.

What I miss besides my parents—my mother is still alive, my father died in 2015—is the food. In my home country and the whole Balkan region, people are always fighting about the origins of their traditional dishes. Serbs will claim something for themselves, Montenegrins, Bosnians, and Macedonians will do the same, and then the Greeks or the Turks will say that the food belongs to them. Well, of course, all that doesn't matter. Balkan cuisine is a mix, and we have it all: moussaka, *dolma, burek.*

My mom cooked everything for us, and she is a very good cook. We ate a lot of cabbage when we lived in Modriča, either growing it ourselves, or buying huge amounts at the market and fermenting them in barrels over the winter. To ferment cabbage, you put it in water and salt, press everything down with a rock, and after a few months, you can take it out and stuff the leaves with meat, rice, and spices. (*Laughs.*)

And then there is *burek*. For us Bosnians, *burek* means pie with meat. There are two ways to make it: like a pizza, but you fry the dough in a lot of oil and then roll it together; or you layer the dough on top of each other. But you always use flaky phyllo dough. I prefer the filling with spinach and cheese, as the meat filling can be a bit heavy. And then there is *ćevapčići*, a homemade grilled sausage; *pljeskavica*, the traditional Serbian burger; and all the pies, pâtés, and breads.

There is a new restaurant not far from here called Balkan StrEAT. It serves Serbian street food and is very good. I have been there three times already. The staff are American, but the chef must be Serbian. One day I will bring you something from there.

JAIRO

I left my hometown, a small town near Puebla, Mexico, when I was twelve years old because my parents decided to bring us to New York. My father came here in 1977, the year I was born. Four years later, he brought my mother. I grew up with my grandparents. My grandfather taught me everything. Life wasn't easy because we didn't have running water, and growing vegetables during the dry season was difficult.

In our town was a *pozo*, a water hole (a well), where everybody went to get their water, with canisters, buckets, or barrels on the back of a pickup truck—whatever they had. People planted corn, watermelons, and *pitaya* to sell, and everybody grew their own food. My grandparents had a small piece of land with some lime and *pitaya* trees, and to grow and harvest our foods there was a wonderful thing. We didn't have much, but we lived a good life.

My grandmother, my mother's mother, cooked wonderful, simple dishes I remember and miss to this day. She used to make *huauzontle*, a vegetable that you marinate, but you need a good recipe and to really know how to make it. My grandmother marinated them with eggs, fried them, and served them in tomato sauce, very similar to chiles rellenos.

I never wanted to leave; my brother did. He really wanted to go to New York, no matter what. So, my father asked me if I wanted to come too, and I said, "Not really." I was happy there. But my brother said, "Hey, let's go. We will make money, and it's a better life over there." I had no choice.

We crossed the border illegally. I was traveling with my brother, cousin, uncle, and his wife, and I was scared because I didn't know anything. The trip to Mexico City took six hours. Then we took a bus to Tijuana, which took three nights and two days. In Tijuana, we crossed. Nowadays they have these big walls, but back then, you could just run. We reached a house, there was a car, and the coyote drove us to Los Angeles.

My father had the contacts from many years ago. Back then, I think it was $1,000 per person. Now it's $8,000 or more. It wasn't that hard. I was young, so I could run. To New York, we took a plane. I got here on the 3rd of July 1990. I remember it because the next day was the 4th of July.

After two years, my father put me in school. I didn't like it. It was difficult to learn. Every week, there was fighting because there were a lot of gangs in the schools of New York. I don't know why. The gangs were not only Mexicans; there were all kinds of people. There were the Latin Kings and the Ñetas from Puerto Rico, the Vatos Locos and Los Cholos from Mexico, and other gangs from other backgrounds. The Mexican gangs came from different parts of Mexico. It's a big country, and people met others from their region and formed a gang, which grew and got bigger and bigger.

They were robbing people. They would take your sneakers, your watch, whatever you have of [value]—anything they can take from you. You saw them hanging around in little groups at street corners. People were scared and tried to avoid them. After a year and a half, I told my dad, "I quit, I can't do it anymore. I want to work. Otherwise, you will see me one day with these people doing something bad, and I don't want that." It was bad, very bad. Leaving school was the only way to escape that world.

I started as a busser at Columbus Bakery on Columbus Avenue. I was sixteen by then and tried to forget everything—my grandparents, my home. I wanted to start my life, and if you keep thinking about the things of the past, it's not good for you. The Columbus Bakery was a very busy place, and Vicki Freeman gave me many opportunities to learn about restaurant work. I will never forget that time.

A few years later, Vicki was thinking about opening a restaurant with her husband, Marc Meyer, and she asked me, "Do you want to work with us?" I said, "Of course, I follow you wherever you go." You opened Five Points in 1999. I've been working for you ever since.

I got my papers in 1993, so every year I would go to Mexico to visit my grandfather. He was like a father to me and such a nice guy. And then, in 1998, he was murdered. I never talk to anyone about this, but . . . (*Pauses.*)

My brother got married in my hometown in 1997, and we stayed there over Christmas and New Year's. When I left, it was so strange. My grandfather had never given me a kiss before. Whenever I left, he always just said, "OK, I will see you again." But that time . . . we said goodbye, and he gave me a hug. We said goodbye three times, and when I sat in the bus, ready to go, my grandfather stopped the bus and came to me, giving me a kiss. He had never done that before. I didn't know it was the last time I would see him, but it was.

I went back to New York on January 10th, 1998, and a few days later they called my father and told him that my grandfather had been kidnapped. They wanted money, so my father got the money and paid. But they wanted more. He got that too, but still they killed him.

We don't know anything about it, but when my brother got married, maybe people were thinking that we had money. It was a small town, and maybe because of all the wine and the food they thought we were rich.

I think my grandfather knew the person who did it, and I also believe that someone in my family was involved. Normally, when they kidnap somebody, they may leave the person bruised, but they don't kill them. They just take the money and let them go. But in my grandfather's case, I think he knew the kidnapper, and that's why they killed him. We never found out what happened or who was involved. The case was closed.

What kept me going was work. And I met my wife at Five Points. She is from Mexico too and grew up just forty-five minutes from my hometown, which is a strange coincidence, no? Our first daughter was born soon after we met. (*Laughs.*) We have two daughters: our oldest is twenty-four and the youngest eighteen. And I'm only forty-five! My wife and I have been together for twenty-four years. I do have my legal documents and papers, but I'm not a citizen yet, not a gringo. (*Laughs.*)

Before my father came here, in 1977, he was working in Mexico like everybody else—a little bit of farming, a little bit of construction, whatever he could find. But it wasn't enough, so he decided to try his luck up north. It was the only chance to create a better life for his family. And he did. We all do. That's why we are here.

My father worked his whole life here as a busser. My uncle was a busser too. Now they are retired. I don't think my father regretted coming here. I don't know when he will go back home. I have three brothers and three sisters; I am the second oldest, and we all live in the US.

I miss my family in Mexico—my father has four brothers and three sisters, and when I still lived with my grandparents, every evening we would be together eating and telling stories and jokes. Everyone would bring a dish—my grandmother would cook some vegetables and *frijoles*, my uncle's wife would make chicken soup, my other uncle's wife would cook mole, and the other uncle's wife would make adobo. We had so many tasty things to eat. I wish we could come back together again one day.

Over there, we didn't have to pay rent, and all the vegetables we planted were organic, fresh, and delicious. I don't plant anything here. My life here, it's just work, work, work.

I'm thinking I might go back. I don't know when, but I'm thinking. We have our own house over there, but nobody lives there anymore. My parents live here in New York; they only go there for vacations. We are five families, and they all live in the US. Our houses in our hometown are empty and in need of repairs.

I watch the news about Mexico all the time. The cartels are everywhere, and when I go to Mexico it's scary because you never know what's going to happen—it's very dangerous. Back then in my town, there was no trouble. You could hang out and go wherever you wanted. But now they've come. You can't deal with these guys. When they come to a small town like ours, they are looking for ways to get money. They watch you, and if they see that you have a good car, a good house, or a nice store, they come to get some money.

But still, I would prefer to be in Mexico. I think I should have stayed. I should have never come to New York. I don't know why I feel like this.

Maybe it's because I left my grandmother and my grandfather alone. They had nobody anymore; we all just left them. I was happy over there, and I think if I would have stayed with my grandfather, what happened to him would have never happened.

When I'm alone, I always ask myself, *Why did we come here?* That question is always with me. Even though I have a whole life here, my wife and my wonderful daughters, who are American with their roots in Mexico, they have both worlds and are smart and educated. I know this, but still . . . why did I come here? Why didn't I stay? I think I lost something from the past, and it's gone forever. I can't get it back.

ONIKA

'm from Trinidad and Tobago, which are like two different places. Tobago is more tourist-oriented, while Trinidad is slightly more urban. I grew up in Trinidad, in Chaguanas, a quiet town surrounded by swampland. In my home country, everything is a little bit slower. Holidays last for an entire week, and Carnival is a big event where no one works for two weeks. People party a lot and go to the beach and the river. They take their "me time" very seriously. (*Laughs.*)

Some of my most special memories from my life in Trinidad are the days at the beach. You would wake up early in the morning and prepare a big pot of something called *pelau*. *Pelau* is rice and beans cooked in coconut milk with chicken. You stew the chicken with brown sugar, add the rice and coconut milk, and let it cook. Then, you add peas and various seasonings, mix everything together, put it in a big pot, wrap it up in sheets and foil, and take it in the back of the truck to the beach, where you spend the whole day.

If you didn't feel like cooking, there were stands at the beach selling *bake* and shark. *Bake* is a fried dough that puffs up, creating a hollow and crispy exterior. Then they fry the shark and place it inside the *bake*, along with grated cucumber, coleslaw, pineapple, and a sauce made with *culantro* and plenty of hot pepper. All of this is done right there at the beach, so you get to eat everything fresh and hot. And yes, it's real shark they fry.

The main beach people go to in Trinidad is Maracas. You drive up a hill along a very narrow road—it's actually scary. When you look down, there is nothing and then comes the water; it feels like certain death! But you take that dangerous hour-long drive because you want your day at the beach. (*Laughs*.) And in case you don't want to go to the beach, you go to the river.

To get there, you would walk through the forest, and on the way, you would notice specific vines growing up the trees. If you followed those vines and pulled them up, you'd find wild yams—root vegetables similar to potatoes. You would gather those yams and some *culantro* along the way, then you would catch a fish in the river and prepare your meal right there using an outdoor burner. It's fantastic; the river, the food, some drinks—everything in Trinidad revolves around food, water, and alcohol. (*Laughs*.)

I have many brothers and sisters because on my mom's side, there were nine siblings, but I didn't grow up with such a large family. I lived with my dad, my stepmother, and one brother. That was my immediate family.

My father came to Trinidad as a young man, from Saint Vincent and the Grenadines, a small Caribbean Island country 150 miles from Trinidad and Tobago. People from smaller islands often move to Trinidad, while people from Trinidad migrate to the United States, Canada, or other places. The interesting thing is that Trinidadians can always tell when you're not from there, even if you come from another part of the Caribbean. I'm not sure why. They claim there's a certain scent or aura that gives it away before you even speak a word.

At first, like most immigrants, my father took on odd jobs nobody else wanted to do, for less pay. But he was ambitious, focused—eventually [he] got into importing and exporting and became a well-known man in Trinidad.

He was very private, quiet, and strict. His primary focus was education. He didn't worry about anything else; education was everything to him. For me, school was tough because I wasn't very social. In school, we spent a lot of time outside. In the mornings, we lined up and sang songs. I was never hungry in school. My stepmother always packed my lunch bag with homemade food. That's how I received her love, because even if you don't communicate well with someone, when they prepare a meal for you, there seems to be a language, an unspoken word in food, don't you think?

My stepmother wasn't unkind or anything, just a little strict, you know? She had an incredible talent for cooking. I believe I inherited my love of cooking from her. She would have me come into the kitchen and let me do everything except the actual cooking. I would wash the dishes, grate the carrots, and assist with various tasks, except for the cooking itself.

Because my father and his wife were very strict, there wasn't much room for self-expression or independence. I didn't have choices when it came to wearing specific clothes, singing songs, or listening to particular music. I remember one time I had an issue of this magazine called *Showtime* that always had a poster inside. This issue came with a Backstreet Boys poster, and I knew my father wouldn't allow me to put it on the wall of my room like you would usually do because it would be me, a young girl, looking at grown men. So, I folded it and hid it in the metal pan in which we carried our geometry tools for school; I put the poster underneath the plastic insert and thought that was very clever and I would be safe. But, oh boy, one random bag check! Bag checks, right? When my stepmother found that poster . . . Well, let's just say the outcome was not exactly pleasant. (*Laughs.*)

I don't know why they were checking my bag. Maybe because I was a young girl in Trinidad, and they couldn't trust us. Because if you're not careful, you could become a statistic, right? You might end up pregnant or something. Those were the prevailing thoughts back then. But honestly, I don't even know when I would have had the time to get pregnant because I was always picked up and dropped off and constantly monitored.

I used to think about leaving Trinidad early in life because, you know, the grass always seems greener on the other side, right? I imagined that in other countries, the grass would be green for most of the year, and then there would be beautiful snow, and you could still walk outside in your pajamas. (*Laughs.*) I had this image from TV shows and movies, where they only showed the nice things. I mean, I wasn't watching something like *Gangs of New York*. (*Laughs.*) I was watching Disney shows.

In Trinidad, American culture was always present—in fashion, movies, and music. And then people would go to work and live in America and there they would pack these big plastic barrels full of food and send them home to their families, and in these barrels, you would have things like Frosted Flakes, large bubble gums, canned foods, flavored peanut butter, and cookies you've never seen before. Of course, people loved it! I mean, if you're eating *cacio e pepe* every day, right? (*Laughs.*)

Anyway, when I was fifteen, I was ready to leave and live somewhere else. Of course, I would have never said that! We didn't have conversations like that. But I was dreaming of a different life. And then one day, my father and my stepmother just came to me and told me that they would send me to the States, to New York, where my mother lived. Just like that. I had just finished my lower secondary level at high school and was about to start the upper, and that's when my father decided to send me to the United States because he believed I would get a better education there. Looking back, I'm not sure if that really worked out. (*Laughs.*)

I came to Flatbush, Brooklyn, and stayed with my mother, who had already been living there for about a decade. I hadn't seen her since she had left, since I was around five years old. So, we reunited after ten years, and my life went from one extreme to another. It went from small-town Chaguanas, Trinidad, to Brooklyn, New York City. It went from living a life where my every move was under scrutiny to a life where I could do what I wanted. My mom had a very different approach to work and education than my father. Hers was more like, "Do what you need to do."

She also had a new family. She had gotten married and had new kids, so when I arrived, I was moving in with people I didn't know at all—and my mom, whom I barely remembered. At first, it was great because all of this brought a sense of freedom. For example, I could go outside and hang out with the kids from the neighborhood, staying out until the sun went down, going to block parties and houses of friends. And I felt welcomed by my new family. I wouldn't say I was loved, but I felt like I was part of something. It all just fell into place, you know? I just didn't feel like I was with my mother. It was more like being with a relative, maybe? Yes, that's how it felt.

I hadn't known much about my mother, but I had one photo of her. In it, she was in a club, had this big, curly hair, and looked fantastic, like a movie star. The way everyone had described my mother to me in Trinidad was that she was wild, that she had worked at bars and clubs, and did whatever she wanted. And that she drank a lot, so yes, I had this idea in my head: she's a rock star, for sure. (*Laughs.*) That's the image I had, based on what people said and that one photo. It didn't really align with the woman I met, though.

When she moved up here, I think her first job was at a bar. But then she started working for this guy named DJ—DJ for Derek Jones. He was a wonderful man and had a small, well-known business in Brooklyn; he basically did garbage removal. Contractors would hire him for demolition and cleanouts. So that's what my mother was doing. She had started as a helper, picking up buckets of trash and such, and eventually moved to working in the office, booking jobs and handling paperwork. I guess you could say she became a foreman. She still had to work and do the heavy lifting, but she also had to handle the paperwork, so she got paid better.

As for my new siblings, they were miserable and annoying. They never listened, never cleaned, and I ended up babysitting them a lot. I remember one time I had a panic attack because they just wouldn't listen. It was the first time I ever experienced a panic attack. My relationship with my stepfather, on the other hand . . . Well, there barely was one. I mean, he was there. I didn't harbor any bad or ill feelings towards him but didn't particularly like him, either. It was fine. We were just coexisting, minding our own business.

That I had lived my whole life on that beautiful island, and suddenly I found myself in the middle of Flatbush, Brooklyn—that drastic change didn't hit me at the time; it was only when I got older. Back then, when I came here, I didn't miss my life in Trinidad at all because Trinidad was synonymous with my father. And Trinidad held a lot of trauma.

Maybe the worst incident happened at our home, and it involved my dad. A couple of years before I left, someone came to our house in Chaguanas. They rang the bell from outside the gate. My stepmother looked and said to my father, "I think it's a Venezuelan guy." Since my father was involved in imports and exports, we didn't find it too strange that he got visited by people from other countries, so we didn't expect anything bad when he went out to talk to the man. And then he got shot, right in front of our house. He was shot and [the man] ran away.

My stepmother quickly moved me and my brother into the bedroom, holding the door shut with her body because we heard people trying to enter the house. They managed to get inside, and we crouched down in a corner while they shot at the bedroom door. The bullet went through, but luckily, it only grazed my stepmother's leg. Then, fortunately, the guys left. We were terribly shocked, of course. My father was in the hospital for months.

When he passed away a few years ago, I went back to that house where the incident happened, our old home, and I felt so sick, scared, and nervous. I was cold-sweating and had to call my husband. I couldn't be in that house anymore. I had to become an adult to understand that I had been traumatized by that experience back then. It was a moment of realization when I realized, "Oh, wow, so that's why I'm a little messed up!" (*Laughs.*)

I never even knew why my father was shot and why we were attacked. Nobody ever gave me the details. But when people ask if I ever missed my home country, I have to say that I didn't start missing it until I was an adult. Until I had to pay my own rent and, you know, just work. I miss the slowness of life there, the good times at the beach. Because up here it's just a hustle, a never-ending hustle. You just work and pay. But for me at the beginning, it was still better than moving back and living there.

I went to school in Flatbush, to Erasmus Hall for business and technology, and for once, I felt like the smartest kid in class. (*Laughs.*) I think my father had this idea that when you go to New York, the education system is going to be so great, and you'll excel. But when I got here, I realized that I had already learned so much; I was beyond the kids in my new class. So I started school thinking, "Nice, this is easy stuff."

Well, that feeling didn't last long, because if you're simply waiting for everyone else to catch up, you stop growing. By the time my classmates were on my level, I had lost my advantage and basically just fell in line with everybody. So yes, I went to Erasmus, joined the basketball club, and got my first job at a sneaker store. That's where I made one really good friend, and we're still friends to this day. I spent time hanging out outside, had a couple of boyfriends—you know, just regular American teen stuff.

After graduating, I went to college and worked with my mother for DJ's rubbish removal company during summer vacations. I remember one time we were doing some work for a guy who had a massive pile of sand he wanted to get rid of. Sand looks like it's something light until you put it in a bucket. The backyard was there, and then there was this long alleyway to the truck; my arms were burning so hard—I swear, I wanted to cry after the first ten trips. I felt like throwing up. But I was working alongside men, the only girl on the job and the only woman besides my mother. And my mother is strong, very strong. (*Laughs.*) So, I knew—you can't cry! You can't complain! You must do the work! That was some tough work, and I did that for some time, working with my mother.

I have a lot of respect for her because she worked really hard. But she was also struggling with alcoholism. It was a combination of working hard from six in the morning until five in the evening and then drinking heavily from five in the evening until late. The times when I saw her at her best were at work. That was the extent of our relationship. I don't hold resentment towards her, though. I think her childhood wasn't easy, and the same goes for her mother's childhood and her mother's mother's childhood. It's like a generational curse, perhaps.

I only know a little bit about my great-grandmother's story. She came from Sicily, Italy, and her family moved to Venezuela. There she met my great-grandfather, who was a Black man. I believe because of that and their interracial relationship, her family saw him as an outcast. So, my great-grandmother left Venezuela with him and moved to Trinidad and Tobago, where she gave birth to a daughter, my grandmother.

I know that my great-grandmother was very hard on her daughter, which seems to be the case with that generation of mothers, but it could be just my family—who knows? Anyway, later, my grandmother married a man in Trinidad and had children with him, but he was very abusive. So, when her youngest child was five, she ran away. And by running away, I mean she truly left everything behind, including her children.

And that created . . . something. I mean, if your mother runs away and leaves you, that does something to children, right? And because his wife wasn't there anymore, her husband picked a child to basically replace her, to address his abuse to, and that was my mother. She was the one. She took on his abuse. And then she ran away too.

I don't know if it's fair to tell her whole story, so I won't. But I understand why she would turn to alcohol. I truly get it. I see it. So, as I got older, my approach to her was kind of like, "I can't really have a close and normal relationship with you, but I don't resent you for what you are right now."

I went to college at John Jay for criminal justice. I wanted to become a lawyer, so I started with a minor in economics and criminal justice. Then, I wanted to pursue prelaw and government, but I couldn't afford to pay the school fees anymore. There simply wasn't enough time to work and earn enough to pay for school while also studying properly, so I stopped somewhere near my junior year with enough credits for an associate degree—and I started working in restaurants.

The first restaurant job I had was at Bake & Things, a Trinidadian restaurant in Flatbush. It mainly focused on takeout. They had a steam table, and people would order food, and I would put it out, bag it up, and give it to them to go. I did that for a while, and then . . . Well, if you go to Park Slope, that area where Prospect Park is, you can start in Flatbush and end up in Park Slope or Kensington. One day, I ended up in the Park Slope part. I had never been in that area before. It's like a whole different world over there. (*Laughs.*) Completely different from Flatbush. I wanted to work as a server, so I walked into this diner; there was this Greek guy, and I said, "I'm looking for a job." He said, "I need a server. Do you have any experience?" I said, "No, but I'm a quick learner." And that was my first full-service job. The diner was called Seventh Avenue Donut Shop. I think it's a historical landmark now. (*Laughs.*)

And it clicked. It's funny. I stayed there until I was pregnant with my first child. I worked there until a couple of weeks before giving birth. I liked that work. I used to meet the most particular customers. For example, I had this guy, a regular, who wanted his toast a specific color, not anything lighter, not anything darker. And there's no button on the machine that you can set for that color. (*Laughs.*) So, I had to stay there and watch and wait until the toast had that specific color so the guy would get it just right. Diner people are the worst! (*Laughs.*) Well, some of them are easy—home fries, sausage, toast, no problem. But others, the eggs need to be specific and perfect the way they like them. The butter must be soft. The coffee must be piping hot or it's not good. It's a lot. But I found that I liked it. I enjoyed talking to them. I liked becoming friends with the regulars. I even liked dealing with grumpy people. Wait, what time is it? (*Checks watch.*) OK, I have to do something in a few minutes.

I've seen all kinds of people. I've seen drifters, I've seen families, I've seen political opponents. I had some terrible customers. I've had people saying the worst things. But mostly it was good. It was fun. And it was good money, especially to start off young. I blew it all on weed and clothes, though. (*Laughs.*) What else are you supposed to do when you are serving and get paid in cash at the end of the day? There were no paychecks. You got everything in cash.

Of course, all that changed with my first child. His name is Marcus—he is going to be fourteen in December. After he was born, I went from diner to diner for a while. I just kind of diner-hopped because they were easy for me. When you work in a diner, there's not a menu you have to study. It's pretty basic, especially Greek diners. They're all serving the same thing.

With the employers in those diners, it was a different story. I found that Greek diners are all family-run, so I didn't have just one boss, one person who owned the restaurant, but multiple bosses; one is a cousin, one is an aunt, another is the mom who needs the bills all facing the same exact way, and the bottle caps have to be put in that special container. She said it was for some kind of donation. But the can tabs, the pieces you flip up? She had us collect those too! (*Laughs.*) So, it wasn't just the customers, but also all those different personalities of my employers. And that was another valuable lesson I learned from working in those Greek diners—how to handle different types of employers. (*Laughs.*)

And then I had another child. I had Michael two years after Marcus. The last diner I worked at was in East New York. One of my former co-workers called me and said, "Hey, these people hired me as a manager. I want you to come over, I need your help." I went there, and that's where I got an eye for management. By then, I had worked in so many diners that I immediately knew, "Yeah, you guys are doing this all wrong."

That area in East New York was in the process of gentrification, so my thought was that you have to change your menu with your population. A diner is a diner, but you must also offer something else for people who don't just want that old stuff. Your new residents, they want a full salad menu, they want different options and toppings, and if they don't want a salad, give them a smoothie. So, I created a whole smoothie menu, I did that myself, and it really took off. I was very proud of that.

Then they had me create the holiday menu, and that was something, because they did a lot of business for holidays, with a lot of take-out orders and so on. You know, diners on holidays are busy, and it's usually a turkey dinner with mashed potatoes and gravy, and we wanted to take that up another notch, so it'd be like lamb and the whole works.

All that was fulfilling. The thing was, I didn't see anything moving past that because they weren't going to make me a manager even though I was taking on all these managerial responsibilities, but there were family members to fill those management roles. So, I made the decision to take charge of my own path, and to do that, I needed to become a legal resident. Up until then, I had simply overstayed my time because my mom had never filed the necessary paperwork for me.

Well, I finally got my working papers and decided to work in a different kind of restaurant, in a different setting, something unfamiliar to me. So, I went to Applebee's. (*Laughs.*) Yes, of all places. But I wanted to work for a big company and see what it was like. It wasn't anything extraordinary, but I did learn a lot about structure. Corporations don't give much room for creativity, but they are very good at teaching structure.

And it was there that I realized that serving no longer worked for me because I needed a more stable income to support my two children. So, I transitioned into my first management job at a restaurant called Hourglass Tavern. It was in a brownstone on Restaurant Row and had three levels, so when you were running food, you went all up and down. (*Laughs.*) I worked there for a couple of years, doing what I enjoyed, and the two owners were incredibly nice, but for the long run they didn't have the number of hours I needed. So, I moved on to Calle Doa, a Cuban-Chinese restaurant, where I started working for five years as a full general manager. Yes, Calle Doa, it means "knife street." (*Checks watch.*) Oh, I really have to go now!

DALILA

I'm from Honduras. I come from a small family. My mom passed away eleven years ago. She was a single mom of four, and I always understood how hard her life was. We lived in a small town in the *municipio* Juticalpa. It's very warm there—all year is summer. I love my town. Everybody knew each other. What else I can say? I'm forty-eight now. So, when I talk about my childhood, I'm talking about forty years ago.

We didn't have much, so we had to make sacrifices to get by. I started taking care of the house and my younger siblings when I was five years old, while my mother and older brother went to work. I was a happy child because my mom never hit me or forced me to do anything. She taught me many things, and when I didn't have shoes, she would make her own shoes smaller so they would fit me, and I wouldn't have to go to school barefoot. She also made her clothes smaller so I could wear them, but I never minded or felt embarrassed. Maybe I'm weird, but I've always thought that you must sacrifice something to get by.

When I finished sixth grade, I wanted to go to middle school, but I realized how expensive the books and the school uniform were. So, I said to my mother, "Mom, I'm ready to work." She said, "Are you crazy?" But I meant it. We had a neighbor, Madrina; she had a business making smoothies and gave me a job. We made the smoothies with oranges, papayas, bananas, strawberries, and apples. We mixed the fruits and added sugar. Madrina paid me eighty *lempiras* per month, less than sixty dollars, but I was so happy because after three months, I had my books and my uniform and started middle school.

My mom always supported my studies, even though she herself didn't believe in school. I think it's because the women in her family never learned how to read and write. They never had the opportunity to learn; they just took care of the house, the husband, and children. That's all they were supposed to do. I didn't like that because I'm going to tell you something: My mom was a kind and smart person. A person that made you think she had read books because of how she set the table, how she said, "Excuse me" and "Thank you." And what did she work as? That's the really sad part. Her main job was cleaning my future college.

She and another lady cleaned the entire building and the backyard. They started at 2 a.m. and had to finish by 6 a.m. because students started coming at 6:30. They worked for the director, who was also the owner of the institute. At some point, the director offered my mother a deal: instead of giving her a vacation and bonus payments, she would let me attend the institute for free. My mother agreed.

I often saw my mother very tired, so I decided to help her. I got up with her at 1:30 a.m., went with her to the college, and helped her clean the place. Then I went back home, quickly took a shower, put on my uniform, and returned. I did this for three years. There were days when my mother couldn't wake up because she was so tired, so I went on my own. I promised her that when I got my degree—I was studying to be a secretary—she wouldn't have to clean the college anymore, and that's what happened. But it almost didn't.

One year before my graduation, I got pregnant. I was seventeen and the father of the child . . . well, it didn't work out. When my mother found out about the pregnancy, she told me, "You have two options: you get married, or you leave the house." I said, "I'm leaving the house." I wasn't going to live with someone who didn't love me. And since I was still a minor, they could have forced him to marry me. So, I left.

That my mother wanted me to leave broke my heart. She didn't talk to me for a week, and I didn't know what to do and where to go—the only support I had was my mother's. So, after that week, I apologized to her and asked for forgiveness. I know it wasn't the right thing to do, but you must understand my decisions. People wanted me to get married, but I wanted to be happy. I told my mother, "If you continue to support me, I promise I will always support you. I will help you if you help me now." That was the pact we made. And I would pay for that a few years later.

Now I continued with my school. It was my last year. The problem was that the institute did not allow pregnant women. But they had evening classes, and that was the only way I could continue my studies—by going at night. You could still attend school if people didn't see you pregnant. It was a small town—everybody knew each other. That's why we were always safe, but also everybody was always worried about what other people said. I never cared about that. I did what I had to do and finished school.

I never thought about aborting my baby, and when my daughter was born, I was so happy. I graduated and got a job at a hotel in my town where I had made my internship. I worked there in customer service, you know, being at the front desk, helping the guests. So I could support her better, my mother suggested that I work double shifts. I agreed, but these double shifts were almost twenty-four hours long. I did that for three months, then I told my mom, who was taking care of my baby, "That's it. I can't do it anymore." My mother had already stopped working at the college, and now we were in trouble because I was so exhausted, I couldn't work for a while and lost my job. At times the money wasn't even enough to buy milk for my daughter.

I had to find a plan B. In our neighborhood, there was a man who owned a store for car parts and supplies. I went to him and asked for a job. He asked me, "What do you know about cars?" I replied, "Everything. I know that wheels are round and keep vehicles moving." He laughed and said, "I'm going to hire you." I worked with regular working hours, from 8 a.m. to 12 p.m. and then 2 p.m. to 5 p.m. However, I was only there for six months because one day someone stole a car battery. The store was crowded, and the other girl who worked there and I had to search for something. That's when the battery got stolen. Since the store was so busy, we couldn't identify who took it. The owner then told me and the other girl that we had to pay for the battery because he couldn't afford to lose the money. I said, "OK, take the money out of my salary, but I'm not coming back anymore." He even came to my mother's house, begging me to return, but I was not going to work for him anymore. I had made up my mind. I was done with him.

And that's when I came across the best opportunity of my life in my country. There was a bank right in front of our house, and they were looking for a secretary, the exact kind of secretary I had been trained for. I got the job and loved it—the work, the salary, my coworkers. But I worked at that bank for only a year and a half. Then, this new journey started—and I came to the USA.

I didn't want to go. I never even thought about it. I had a future in Honduras, a really good one. I loved my life there. Just the month before I came here, there was a construction company offering houses [to] all the bank employees with low interest rates for a minimum of thirty years to pay off the loan. And my income gave me the opportunity to fix my mom's house, to renovate it—it was fantastic. I had money, I could help my mother, I was about to have my own house soon.

Around that time, one of my mom's friends offered my sister the opportunity to come to the USA. She was supposed to work in New York for a woman from Honduras who imported Honduran products like chorizos and cheeses. My sister enthusiastically said yes but then changed her mind at the very last minute. So, my mother convinced me to take my sister's place instead.

I didn't want to go. Even the bank manager told me, "Dalila, don't go! If it's about money, we can lend you some. You can open your own business, but don't go!" I replied, "But I have to." I didn't have any other words. Here's how my mother convinced me: She said, "You'll make more money over there, you'll be able to help us more, and one day you'll come back and have your own house here. But for now, you need to go."

Suddenly, I was in New York while my daughter stayed in Honduras with my mother. I have been living here for twenty-seven years now, in the same neighborhood, in Jamaica, Queens. My beginnings here were bad. The job from that lady from Honduras seemed like a good opportunity, but she ended up basically abusing me and taking advantage of my situation.

This woman wanted Hondurans in the US so she could pay them in *lempiras*, the Honduran currency, which was worth close to nothing. I was treated as cheap labor, almost like a slave. I had to live with other workers in her house, paying rent to her—way too much, as I realized later—and I was getting sick from the work. The job was to sell these Honduran products to Hondurans. It was all under the table, and there were these fumes, vinegar and other things.

It took me six months to pay back for my trip. My mother and daughter survived that time because my manager at the bank had paid me all my vacation days and bonuses, even though I didn't give enough notice before leaving. I had given that money to my mom. After six months, she started complaining, and of course I immediately started sending her the little that woman paid me. I didn't realize how much that woman took advantage of me. I was blind, totally blind.

I had to go to the emergency room many times because of the fumes or the stress. I don't know what caused it, but I had a lot of reactions all over my body. One day at the hospital, I met a guy who was one of the renters in the woman's house. He looked at me and said, "You are stupid. She's using you. Don't do it."

He opened my eyes. He was also from Honduras. He made me understand that this woman liked to have people from our country because that way she could control them better and nobody realized what she was doing. I had never lived by myself. And then God sent me that angel, that guy.

I fell in love with him. He took me from that place. He said to me, "You're not going to work for her anymore." And he moved away from there too. We started a relationship, and he told me, "Don't worry, there are many opportunities in this country." And that's when I started my real life here.

He taught me how to take the train and the bus and started teaching me many things. And I didn't speak a single word of English. (*Laughs.*) I found a job in housecleaning and started becoming very independent, thanks to him. He was a good guy. I cleaned houses all over New York, in Staten Island, Manhattan. My guy was working in restaurants, and one day I said to him, "I also want to work in a restaurant." He replied, "Yeah, but it's hard. It's very difficult because people must be tough—you're not going to handle it." So, I kept cleaning houses for fifteen years.

You know what's the weird part? I never cleaned my own home. I don't know why, but I never swept the floor, never washed the clothes, nothing. I did that only for other people. For them, I was the best, and I loved it—it was my job. There was very good money in that too because they pay you in cash, but of course without benefits. If you didn't work that day, you didn't get paid.

After three years, I got pregnant with our son. And six years after that, I got pregnant with my little one. She's seventeen now. During all that, the guy and I got separated because he had a lot of issues. He had accidents in his job, and it was a lot of sacrifice for me because I had to support my family here in New York, my family in Honduras, and him. And then, you know, sometimes people change. He changed. He hit me a lot. We separated, and for nine months, we lived in the same apartment but in separate rooms. I had two children with him. As for me, I have gratitude. And maybe that's why I always supported him because when I needed it, he had been there for me. He had taken me away from that place and that woman. He wasn't a bad guy. But people change, you know? People change.

The third time my mother broke my heart was when she told me that she couldn't take care of my daughter anymore. My daughter was fourteen years old, and I was here in New York. The problem was that my brother had started living with my mother as well, and he and my daughter didn't get along. So, my mother told me, "I can't help you anymore with your daughter. You have to find a place for her." My daughter was fourteen years old. Her name is Osiris.

She told me on the phone, "Mommy, Grandma doesn't want me anymore. But I have a friend—she said she can take care of me. You must send her money for the food, my college, and everything." And that's how Fany came into our lives.

My mom and Fany's mom were really close friends. How small our town was! I also knew Fany's mom, but I had never met Fany because she was nine years old when I left. And now she was friends with my daughter, found an apartment for her and two of her friends, and took care of them—these three girls who went to college. Fany helped a lot of people in our town. A lot. But back then, I didn't know anything about her.

When my mom told me that my daughter had to leave, I told her, "OK, you choose your son, I'm going to choose my daughter. That's it for me. Don't expect any more money from me." So, I cut her off and started supporting my daughter solely. And thanks to Fany it all worked out.

Two years later, my daughter was sixteen and wanted to come here with her two friends. I didn't like the idea because it's such a hard trip and everything, but Osiris insisted. She had made up her mind. The problem was, by then I was already nine months separated from the father of my two kids here, and I needed him to deal with the coyotes. That always had to be done by a man. And can you believe it? He charged me for that! Well, at least he was doing it. I had to collect almost $10,000 for the girls' trip. I had to pay for boats and such. Thank God everything went well, and nothing bad happened.

Exactly one month after my daughter came, my mom passed away. It was difficult for me, even though she had let me down many times.

My daughter stayed with me for just one month. Then one day she came home with a boyfriend and left. Just like that. My daughter! Well, I let it go. She was young, and after two months, she returned to me because the relationship with that guy wasn't good. But then she went back with him again! She played around like that for a while until one day I said, "No more." She is a strong-willed girl and a hard worker. Now we have the best relationship. Osiris is thirty years old now—can you believe it? (*Laughs.*)

During the time my daughter came to New York, that's when I met Fany—on Facebook. And that's how Fany came into my heart. We have been together for eleven years now, and we are a family. I think it was in 2013 when Fany told me, "Dalila, you can't do this job anymore, this housecleaning. You can do better. Go to restaurants. You can handle it. You'll be fine." I still had the words of my ex in my ears, that it would be too tough for me, but I trusted in Fany, and that's how I started, after fifteen years of housecleaning.

I owe a lot to Chef Margot, who believed in me and gave me the opportunity. I did prep, then I cooked breakfast for a year and a half, from 5:30 a.m. to 12 p.m. I was good at that, I loved it. I never missed a day, and I was really enjoying my life.

Then the pandemic came, and I was sitting there, having nothing to do, and I started dreaming. Because for many years, I never dreamed of something. I had left my dreams in my country. But now they returned, and I sat down with Fany and told her, "Fany, I want to study childcare." So, I was looking until I found an opportunity here in Queens, where I could learn it. And last week I graduated!

I graduated with a degree in childhood development, and I can also work as an assistant teacher. I was never so excited before. Because [of] my age—I'm forty-eight years old now . . . I had to start learning and writing English. It's so hard. But I did all this. And all this I dedicate to my children, to Fany, to myself, to my family. And if I don't get this dream, I'm going to continue dreaming.

ANGEL V.

I'm from Caracas, Venezuela. Growing up was wonderful. I had a happy childhood in a huge family, with two brothers and many cousins. As a child, I didn't feel any political turmoil. For me, it all started with the government they installed after Chávez's death in 2013, the one with Maduro, the one we still have now. I was fifteen then, and it was with this government that I started to become more aware of the political situation in my country. The same political situation that, thirteen years later, made me move to the United States.

There were riots in the streets, and the government was cracking down on students and anyone who was not happy with their rule. I was a student activist and worked for one of the big opposition political parties in Venezuela, and they started targeting me and my family, particularly my mom. It was a difficult situation. I was kidnapped twice, and the second time was really scary.

The first time I was eighteen years old. I had just joined a local party for young people and was filled with joy. It was exactly what I had been searching for—a breath of fresh air, something new, an outlet for the energies released by my political awakening. It felt as though I had spent my entire life trapped in a cycle—first, Chávez held all the power, and things started to deteriorate. Then came Maduro, and the situation worsened. With my political work, I had found a way out of my powerlessness, and I really believed in change, that we could make it.

My family was middle class when that word, that concept, still held some meaning. Before Chávez, we were doing fine. I used to travel with my parents to the United States for vacations two or three times a year. Under Chávez, we couldn't do that anymore. Maybe just once a year, and we had to save up for it. But what really worried me was when the sense of security disappeared. It became unsafe to go anywhere, especially at night. The police were involved in robberies and kidnappings, and corruption was widespread. I started to ask myself, "Why is this happening?" I wanted answers. I wanted change.

I spent most of my teenage years with my friends at my house. Parties, birthdays, just hanging out—everything happened there because we had the biggest house. We lived in a well-situated suburb, and when I visited a friend in the city, I had to stay overnight because my mom didn't want me to come back at night. It was too dangerous even for her or my dad to pick me up.

When I got older, I didn't mind not being able to go out anymore. But I did mind realizing that I wouldn't be able to afford buying a house like my parents did when they were younger or just living a normal life. The money we earned was practically worthless due to the high inflation. Life became increasingly difficult, and the future looked bleak. That's why I started being an activist, and that's why I had to leave.

My grandmother, my mother's mother, was the head of the family, the matriarch. She was always busy, cooking, selling food to the neighbors, sewing clothes and bags, and working as a teacher. Her husband had left her when my mother was fourteen, so my grandmother always needed to find ways to get by. Her days would begin at four in the morning and end around midnight. She is one of the hardest workers I know. My father's side of the family was much better off.

I have two favorite dishes from my grandmother. One of them is *asado negro*, one of the most traditional Venezuelan dishes. It is an eye of round roast that is slow cooked in a slightly sweet and incredibly flavorful dark sauce, a very complex and time-consuming meal. She usually cooked it on Saturdays, and we would have it for Sunday lunch.

My other favorite is *hallacas*, a kind of tamale that we make in December, and it is my favorite because of its taste, of course, and because it brings the entire family together. It takes so many hands to make it! (*Laughs.*)

Hallacas are made with cornmeal, and the stew that goes inside includes pork, beef, and chicken, all cut into squares. We also use this block of brown sugar that my grandmother . . . used for the *asado negro* sauce—it's called *papelón* and you grate it. My grandmother always said that every dish needs a touch of sweetness. And she used these sweet mole peppers called *aji dulce* for the stew. We used to get them from Margarita Island, where we have family, because the best and most aromatic ones grow there. They have a strong and pleasant aroma and are never spicy.

Preparing the fillings and sauces for the *hallacas* was a lot of work. Each one of us had our station and specific job. As a child, my task was to boil the banana leaves to get them soft. My grandmother was in charge of the stew. Nobody else was allowed to handle it. She said that if someone else touched it, it would go bad. (*Laughs.*) We have a saying: "*Muchas manos en el caldo, lo pone morado.*" Many hands in the broth, turns it purple.

When everything was prepared, my grandmother would pass the open *hallaca* around, and we would all put our ingredients inside or do our designated tasks. The person at the end of the line, usually the head of the household—namely, my father—was responsible for folding the *hallaca* in a banana leaf and sealing it.

When I was a child, my grandmother used to make so many *hallacas* at the end of the year that everyone would get a generous share. If you were a family of three, you would get fifty *hallacas*. If you were a family of six, you would get a hundred. And she always had extra stock to give to neighbors.

But with the deterioration of the country, the quantity of *hallacas* started to decrease because it became more and more difficult to get the necessary ingredients. When I was a child, we used to make five hundred *hallacas*. The entire refrigerator would be filled with them. Around the time I was fifteen, we were down to just one hundred.

That's when it started to get bad. My parents were working more and more to pay the mortgage and the car, and everything was getting a little bit harder all the time. Everything was becoming increasingly difficult. We were middle class, and at some point, the middle class in

Venezuela just stopped existing. This is what's left of the middle class nowadays: You are either really, really rich to sustain your living, or you are poor like everybody else in this country, but you have somebody living and working abroad who is sending you money. Like I am here in the United States, and I'm taking care of a huge part of my family back in Venezuela. We are three now here: my mother, my little brother, and me. We work and have our monthly budget, and the rest we send to our family.

I never wanted to leave. I never even thought about it, not even after I got kidnapped for the first time. I got kidnapped both times because of my activism. The first time, I think they just wanted to scare me. And they did, at least for a while. I didn't leave the house for three months. I was doing things from home, though, helping wherever I could, but then I thought, "I must go back. I have to be myself again. It's important to be more helpful." So, I went out again.

Part of my activism was to go to poor neighborhoods with a local oppositional party to help people, see what they needed, and figure out what could be done. I spoke to people who hadn't eaten for days, but they were still content with the government. So, you tried to make them understand that whatever was happening to them was not fair. That we are a rich country, that we have petroleum, that we used to be one of the wealthiest countries in Latin America.

In the past, people from Venezuela never wanted to live somewhere else. People from other countries came to us to see how we were doing it, why we were so good! Our subway system, for example, was very innovative in South America. We had a very modern hydroelectric dam and so on. I know all this because I read a lot, but all that happened before my time. I only know the country is getting worse and worse. I saw the city start to fall apart. The train services, the highways . . . Bridges were collapsing. We started having problems with electricity, and people's food went bad in their fridges.

When I got kidnapped for the first time, I was eighteen and on my way to the university where I studied law. They held me for one night and told me things like, "We know what you are doing." They just wanted to scare me. But when they kidnapped me for the second time, my family got involved.

I was twenty-eight, and this time they had information about my parents. They knew my father's name, the times my mother left the house, where she worked, and other details. This really frightened me. I didn't want anyone in my family to get hurt because of what I believed in. Although my family shared my beliefs, they repeatedly told me, "Don't go to that march," or "Don't talk about that so openly, don't make yourself so public." I tried to be cautious, but sometimes it just happened. So, when they kidnapped me for the second time, they said, "You have to stop. We know your mother. We know your little brother." My little brother was six years old at that time, and they knew where he went to school.

By that time, I was more involved than before. I was close to popular people in opposition parties, political leaders who were taken to jail for no other reason except that they were opposing the government, which was basically seen as an invitation to war.

The last political party I worked with was Voluntad Popular, also known as Popular Will, a party dedicated to democratic reforms, human rights, and social justice, with Leopoldo Lopez as its face and leader. And then he was put in jail; he got imprisoned for many years. Everybody had already been whispering that these kinds of things could happen, but when it happened, it was still a shock. He was one of the biggest oppositional leaders and the mayor of Chacao, a municipality in Caracas. You never thought they would go against people like that just because they were against the government. And then they did.

I've heard that since 2015, around six million Venezuelans have left the country. I didn't want to—I always had hope that things would get better. But after my second kidnapping, my mother was really worried about me, and I was worried about my family. So, I left.

I thought I was going to stay here for a maximum of six months; I didn't want to get in trouble with overstaying my visa and was planning to go back for my birthday. But then my mom started getting calls again, and one night she called me and told me that someone had been following her on a motorcycle. In Venezuela, many bad things happen with people on motorcycles, and this guy had followed her all day. She said, "I don't think it's a good time for you to come back."

I applied for political asylum and started looking for work. I was a lawyer back in Venezuela, but I wasn't allowed to practice here. A friend told me that the best way to start was in the restaurant business. He said that restaurants are always helpful to people who are just starting out. I didn't know anything about this world, neither the kitchen nor the service, but I was open to learning.

First, I worked as a dishwasher. (*Laughs.*) It was the best job for me because my English wasn't good. I washed dishes in different places, but it was so hard. I think it's the hardest work, and now that I work in the industry, I know that besides preparation, it's also the work we need the most in the back of the restaurant to keep everything running.

The back of a restaurant works like the mechanism of a clock. If one piece isn't functioning well, the clock will stop. When I was a dishwasher, the chef in one of the restaurants saw me and asked, "Are you interested in being part of the kitchen?" And like that, I got many chances and opportunities until I eventually worked in the front of the house.

I worked as a busser, then as a runner. I paid attention to what was going on. If a customer said, "Can I have some more *croquetas*?" I would say, "Table 19 wants more *croquetas*." I would get the information to the server, which helped the server. Then one of the servers said to me, "Hey, I'm busy. Can you go to that table and take their order?" I said, "Sure," and took the order. I was starting to get more confident, and at some point, my manager gave me a job as a server.

That manager was like my father here in the US. He taught me many things, sometimes with a hard hand, but he showed me his love after I got better, after I proved myself. I got better shifts and started helping him more and more with his job. I was helping with the inventory and in charge of dividing the tips for the servers at the end of the night. The more things he gave me to do, the more I learned.

At the beginning, it was hard, of course. I'm a lawyer. I want to practice. I want to do the things I studied for. But working as a server seemed to be the best that I could do here. I've been working in the industry for seven years now. It's hard work, but it's good money. In Venezuela, I would never have had the chance to save, help my family, and get a car, an apartment, things like that. And at some point, I just stopped thinking about going back.

I'm thirty-five now and a New Yorker. Well, okay, I've been here for seven years, so I have to wait three more years to be a real New Yorker. (*Laughs.*) But I love New York City. I might move to the suburbs one day or to New Jersey or a different state to have more of a home because, of course, New York is always chaos and rush and all. Long-term, I want to have a small restaurant where I can show people all the good things I remember from my grandmother—a good, small family business, nothing too big. Something that my mom could do with me, and my grandmother can be involved in when she visits us. I guess the restaurant business got under my skin. (*Laughs.*)

I got all of this from my mom—like being positive and outgoing and hoping for the best. Also, church still plays a role in my life. My family is moderately religious, and I'm still going to church because there I feel a connection with people who are no longer with me, and I feel a connection with God. I go and I pray, and of course not everybody likes this because I'm openly gay. Not everyone in my family was happy about that either, but I think I showed them that being gay doesn't have anything to do with who I am. I'm still Angel, their son, the person they know and [who] had to leave because of his beliefs and found a new life in this big, loud, vast, wild city. And I feel my family respects me for that.

MOUSTAFA

I'm from Alexandria, Egypt. I grew up on the beach, catching fish and octopus and hanging out with my friends. I had one of these typical dads of that time—very loving and caring but not open to discussions. When he came home in his car, we ran away, like, "Oh no, Dad is here!" (*Laughs.*)

He was an engineer and owned a construction company, while my mother was taking care of the house and the family—very old-school. They stayed together for fifty years, until he passed away. We lived in a safe neighborhood, upper middle class, and for the most part my childhood was a happy one, but I had a rough youth. I had access to money and time, and that sometimes leads you down the wrong path, and that's where I went. I used to take a lot of drugs between the ages of fourteen and eighteen.

A lot of this stuff was available, even [with] Egypt being a conservative country. The police were looking the other way. The government didn't mind either; I'm sure they encouraged the situation to keep people tame and asleep. For us at this age, it was all about staying up all night and sleeping all day, until things got too bad, and we decided to stop. To do so, we had to separate. Ultimately, that's why I left, because of the drugs. It had nothing to do with the political situation. I just didn't want to disappoint my parents. I didn't want to break their hearts. But before I left my dad made sure I [got] my accounting degree.

I went to New York right away. I was twenty by then, my English was fair, and I knew one person, a friend of my father, who helped me to get my first job at a clothing store called Portabella in Jamaica,

Queens. It was one of these African American fashion-forward places with long suits, gator shoes, and high-tops. The customers were easy with me, sharing smiles and jokes, especially when they learned that I'm Egyptian: "Ah, you are from the motherland, from Africa!" They dropped a lot of money there—$600 for a pair of gator shoes, $3,000 for five suits at once, and I made a 10 percent commission, so one big sale and I was good for the day. Good times. Until they decided to move me to a different location. The owner, an Egyptian from my hometown, had thirty-five of these stores, and I got upset that they were moving me somewhere else without even asking me, so I quit, kind of shooting myself in the foot because that was one good job.

The easiest thing for me at the time was to become a busboy. That was my first step towards the kitchen, but I never thought I would become a cook one day. I was just a kid stumbling around, trying to make a living. I worked at this barbecue joint on Greenwich and 7th Avenue, across the street from St. Vincent's Hospital. Then 9/11 happened, and the restaurant closed because it was very close to the site. To get by, I did deliveries on a bike. I always knew one thing: I came here on my own, and nobody will take care of me, so I have to earn my dinner. Of course, I didn't let my father know what I was doing for a living, [so as] not to upset him. He wouldn't have been happy knowing that his son, the one with the accounting degree, was delivering noodles on a bike in New York. (*Laughs.*) I did that for a year, then they had cleaned and reopened the restaurant, and I returned and became a food runner.

My kitchen career started on a Saturday night. There were four hundred reservations for dinner, and the salad guy didn't show up for work. The kitchen was open, and I was standing there, watching the plates come up. I told the chef, "Listen, you have two choices. Either you are screwed or you let me in. That way, you might be screwed too, but you never know." Two hours later, the owner walked in and said: "You are in the kitchen? I'm going to make you one even better. You'll still get your check from the floor, and you'll get paid from the kitchen, but you stay in the kitchen." And that was it. I never looked back from that day.

What made me love the kitchen is—and it sounds like an asshole thing to say—but it's the amount of power that cooks have. I don't mean to be dismissive to service staff, but cooks work with knives and fire! (*Laughs.*) And I used to collect knives, since I was five. So, when I started that night when the salad guy didn't show up, it was like a drug, my second drug, honest to God. The adrenaline! The push, the rush, the food, the meticulous attention to detail! I always thought of it as a factory, where every burger has to come out of my hand the same way every time, down to the salad leaf. But, of course, I didn't want to be flipping burgers for the rest of my life. You want to be better. There is just so much more.

Before I got into cooking, I couldn't even boil an egg without burning it. I didn't know salt from pepper, nothing, zero. I was just a stupid little kid running around New York, but I wanted to do better. I wanted to make my parents proud. I couldn't fail; I was stubborn in this regard. Everything I've ever done as a cook comes from there. I always made sure that my next job was on a little higher level or at least a different cuisine. From French to American to Mexican to Italian.

Before I worked for Chef Ayesha and the Bowery Group, I worked for the Employees Only company that owns the famous cocktail bar EO. Here I learned all about cooking food and assembling dishes. At first, I was just a line cook, but in beast mode. (*Laughs.*) I love working on the line—I sweat, it's like working out, I feel my body is getting something done. That's my therapy; it puts me in a zen mode, makes me happy. Then they wanted me to be a sous chef. I stayed with them for four years and loved every minute of it. They gave me my wings.

When I wanted to move, they offered me a job at Walter Foods in Williamsburg; they kind of ran in the same circles. It was my first solo. It wasn't a head chef position since the place was small, but it was cranking, one of the busiest places in Williamsburg. At first, I was very scared. I kept thinking, "What if I kill somebody? I don't know what I'm doing!" But I always told myself, "You wake up, you do what you have to do, so just be on time and careful with every step you take." That's how I calmed myself. I guess it worked. I stayed at Walter Foods for four years, then Employees Only reached out to me again because they wanted to open a place in Miami and made me a small partner. Well, that didn't work out . . .

First, I was in logistics, managing the construction. But it's very tricky to build anything in Miami, especially on the beach, because everything is historically preserved. You have to apply for everything, even to put a nail in. The construction took us a good seven months, then we opened. It was the same menu as up here in New York—kind of American with a Balkan twist, because the owners were from Serbia and Bosnia. The first months, we did fantastic. We opened in February and were busy every night, doing one-fifty, two hundred [thousand dollars] a week, and actually broke even for a minute—then came summertime. You know, Miami at the beach, it's like the flip of a switch. We changed the menu, cut costs where we could, until it was only me and another guy in the kitchen, but nothing helped, and I felt like I didn't have an answer for this situation. So, I asked them to let me go and save my money. I needed to go home to regroup. And when I say "home," I mean Egypt. When I came back to Miami—well, that's stuff I don't want to get into. Anyway, it ended down there, and the guys at Walter Foods had a lousy chef, so I came back to New York and stayed with them for a couple of years.

Then I had a little adventure in Poland. I went there for six months and opened a company that exported and imported fruits and vegetables from Egypt to Europe. Then the pandemic came and wiped out everything. (*Laughs.*) There was a shipment of oranges that got stuck at sea, because everything just got closed—all the borders and harbors. Eventually, all the oranges got thrown into the water, and that was that. Luckily, I was here in New York and got my job with Chef Ayesha, so I was good and back in the kitchen. And that's where I met my wife when I was forty-seven. I told my mom that I was going to get married, and she just said, "Finally!" (*Laughs.*)

Of course, some part of me always missed Alexandria, and that homesickness never really goes away. But it's not as bad now as it used to be back then when I started here. You put down roots where you stay, so my life is here now. And sometimes when I go back home, I miss New York. It's a limbo. It's the immigrant life—you are always missing something. When you're home, you miss your second home; when you are at your second home, you miss your first.

I remember many wonderful dishes my mother used to make. She was a good cook, one of the best, but if I hung out in the kitchen, she would always kick me out. (*Laughs.*) One of my favorites is a Greek dish—pastitsio with bechamel sauce. Not moussaka—that's made with eggplant. My mom's version uses penne pasta layered with ground beef in the middle, and then she makes a bechamel sauce and bakes it all. It's quite popular in Alexandria, maybe because there have always been a lot of Greeks there.

And then there was *molokhia*—it's made with a green leaf called Jew's mallow. You chop it and cook it with chicken stock or shrimp stock, and then you toss garlic and coriander on top—I can swim in that stuff. And anything my mother pickled, like stuffed eggplants . . . I'm getting hungry, with a tear in my eye. (*Laughs.*)

LUIS

I am from Ecuador, from a small town five hours from the coast. We were a poor family, but I never wanted to leave my country—never even thought about it. I came to the United States because my oldest brother, Diego,* had tried to come here and failed. He went from Ecuador to Nicaragua, where immigration arrested him. For two months, he was in some kind of camp, and when he came back home, he was very sick. The problem was that he and my mother had borrowed money to pay for his trip, and now they had to pay that money back.

My mother was crying for days. So, I said to her, "Mom, I will go to the USA and make the money, don't worry." She replied, "What are you talking about? You are a kid; you just finished school." I was fifteen, but I always thought of myself as a strong guy; when I was kid, I even called myself Hercules. (*Laughs.*) I told her that I was stronger than my brother, that I was her Hercules. It took me a week to convince her. I just wanted to make her stop crying and wasn't thinking about the fact that I would be leaving my country, my family, my friends—everything.

I left my country in January 1999 and haven't seen my mother since. That's the hardest part—waking up every day in a life without her. I left and made it in just twenty days. I went from Ecuador to Peru, and there I took a boat. The coyotes had told me that I was going to take a plane from Peru to Mexico, but I ended up on that boat with seventy other people. It was a fishing boat that traveled from Peru to Guatemala. I spent eight days and nights on that boat. That was the toughest time of

---

* See Diego's story on page 141.

my journey because I didn't eat for a couple of days, and being on the water is . . . Well, you only see water. It's like you are in the same spot for days. But I wasn't scared; I was happy. I was the youngest, and they called me "*el niño*," the boy.

At some point, something broke on the boat in the open water. What had happened was that the boat went over a giant turtle, and the turtle shell broke something, causing the boat to tilt to its side, and all the water was coming on top of us. People were freaking out, scared that we might die. But I was like, "No problem, I can swim." (*Laughs.*) I didn't think about the fact that I was in the middle of the ocean. I wasn't scared at all.

My life in Ecuador was very happy, though I only realized that later. As a kid, growing up, you sometimes don't think your life is great because you see other kids whose parents have cars and everything they need. We were poor. My father was an alcoholic. I didn't even get a bicycle until I was ten, and I pretty much had to build it myself. Back then, I didn't know I was lucky to be born where I was and to have what I had. I didn't know that was the most beautiful life and time I'd ever have. But I did know I was happy. I was a joyful boy all the time, and I had lots of friends.

When I left, I wanted to be a hero. I wanted to be my mom's hero. I didn't realize that it would be my last time with her and everybody else. Even when I was crossing, I was happy. The people I was with were like, "Hey, calm down, stop jumping around. This is not a trip we're doing for fun." (*Laughs.*) I wasn't afraid or worried—I was just having a good time. But when I woke up in this country, the first time waking up in the United States, I immediately wondered, "How am I going to get home now?" Where were my mom, my sisters, my friends? On the second day I realized what I had done. All I wanted was to go back.

After we arrived in Guatemala [in] the boat from Peru, we crossed to Mexico. I hadn't eaten for days, and they told us we would go to a house and get two tortillas and a coffee, and as we got closer, I could smell them; they smelled like the corn tortillas from home. But the tortillas they gave us were thin like paper, not like the thick ones I knew.

Now I love them, but back then I was very disappointed by the Mexican tortillas. (*Laughs.*)

We walked through Mexico, mostly at night; during the day, we rested. Only once did we go on a small bus, but I don't know how far—I fell asleep. I was very lucky; I made it to the States in twenty days. One of my cousins left around the same time as me, and it took him two months. We crossed the border on foot and were already in Texas when Immigration caught us. There were sixty people in one room in a house, and when I woke up, there were flashlights everywhere. But because I was underage, they didn't send me back; instead, they put me on a plane to New York after five days, where I had an uncle who helped me with a lawyer.

In New York, I fully realized what I had done—how far away I was from my family. That thought destroyed me. I spend weeks and months crying every night. It got so bad that my uncle even considered sending me back. I overheard him talking on the phone with my mom about it. And yes, I could have gone back, but then who would have paid the money for my brother's trip and mine? It took me about three years to repay that money. Three years of work, just to pay back the money for our trips!

I only knew my uncle in this country. He lived in Queens. My first job was as a dishwasher in an Italian restaurant with five floors on 53rd and Lexington. I was there for three months. Then I found another job at San Pietro near 5th Avenue. There I only washed dishes for a month, because I always loved the kitchen, so I'd wash the dishes as fast as I could to then run over to the salad station and help the guy. The chef, who was also the owner, watched me and asked, "What are you doing?" I said, "I'm helping the salad guy." That happened a couple of times and he would get mad until he finally gave me the chance to be a salad guy, and from the salad station I rushed over to help the cooks, the chef watching. He was a scary sight, this big Italian guy. And he was always screaming. But I was never afraid of him because I knew I was only helping. He ended up liking me, saying that I was his son. I moved from station to station and learned a lot in this restaurant. At the end I was making the pastas. I worked there for almost two years, until the chef didn't pay me correctly and I left.

After that—by then I was seventeen years old—I moved to Connecticut, where one of my cousins lived. I worked in a restaurant there, eleven hours a day, six days a week, for $275 a week. Until my cousin said, "Listen, I can get you a busboy job for $500 a week, and you would work half the time." The problem was, I didn't want to leave the kitchen. I told him, "I want to be a chef!" My cousin said, "But you came here to make money." He was right. So, I worked as a busboy, only half the time and making almost double. Did it for two years, then moved back to New York. And that's when I met my wife. We were both twenty years old.

Back then I talked to my mother only once a week. There were no video calls like today—we could only keep contact through expensive phone calls and letters, and for every phone call my mother had to drive to the city because my parents didn't have a phone back then.

In Connecticut I put away my dreams of being a chef, because I had to make money. But it's not too late. I still want to do it. My big dream is to open my own restaurant one day. To bring everything together with what I've learned in all these years. I don't want it to be Ecuadorian food or Mexican or Colombian. I want to have everything, all at one place. For all kind of people. If you want to eat pasta, I can make you pasta. And I will make something for the kids. I dream of a restaurant for everybody.

I miss my mother, and I miss her food. My favorite dish was spaghetti with tuna. She would make the sauce with tomatoes, onions, potatoes, and canned tuna. I still make it for my kids. We call it "grandma's pasta." They think it's really good. (*Laughs.*) And [I] loved her *seco de pollo*, a traditional Ecuadorian dish. It's basically chicken stew, served with rice, red peppers, cilantro, garlic. That and the *cuy*, the guinea pig. But that's for special occasions. They get roasted on a stick over a fire. Pretty much everybody in Ecuador likes *cuy*. It's very expensive. I used to [raise] them. Taking care of them was part of my job back then, when I was a kid. There was good money in [raising] guinea pigs.

One of my aunts sold food in the city in a small food stand and used to make *fritada*, pork with dry *maiz*—you fry it for a long time in its own grease so it's nice and crispy. It's also called *chicharron.* My other aunt used to make soups, like minestrone. She used beans, potatoes, cabbage, and she would add bones of pork—that's why we called it *sopa de pobres,* poor people's soup. Well, we were poor. My shoes were open on the side, there were holes in the front, my pants were all ripped, but I never went to bed hungry. I think my mom did. She often said she had enough and gave me her dinner. That went on until my brother Diego told me what was going on, that she just did it for me, so I would never stay hungry.

I knew the special tastes of the foods of each of my aunts. And they used to love me because I was a food lover even as a kid. Whatever they gave me, I always said: "Gracias!" I never said no. (*Laughs.*) Later, one of my aunts had an Ecuadorian restaurant here in New York, and that's where I met my wife, who worked there as a server. Now we have four kids. My oldest is seventeen, the youngest four. They make me cook for them. If I cook pasta I have to cook four different versions: pink, white, with meat, and without. (*Laughs.*) I love doing that. It makes me happy. Some years ago, my wife stopped working to take care of our home and the kids. I have two jobs, I always have, but I'm aware that her work is actually harder than mine.

Here at Cookshop, I started as a runner, then I became the expeditor for seven years, and now I am a server. I really loved being an expeditor because I got to deal with food, and that's something I really like. Often, I would jump into the kitchen, put on a chef coat, and help. I think I can do anything in the kitchen, at every station. The only reason I don't work as a cook is the money. As a server, I just make more.

The idea of going back to Ecuador and living there died a couple of years ago. In the beginning, I wanted nothing more than to go back, but when you have four kids, you erase all those dreams and only think about what's good for them, until they are grown up and start living their own life. And by that time, well, maybe I'll go back to Ecuador to die in peace. (*Laughs.*) But for now, I want to live my life here as well as I can. Plus, the situation in my home country is even worse today. Even the people changed—they don't work that hard anymore.

Because if you live there, you won't achieve much in your life, no matter how hard you work or what you do. Whether you're a teacher, lawyer, or a businessman—your money won't stay in your pocket for long. Building a house or getting a car, especially with a family, becomes nearly impossible. That's why nowadays, so many people try to come here. Even those who've earned money in the US and returned to Ecuador don't want to stay there anymore. My cousin earned enough to go back to Ecuador, where he opened his own restaurant. He even has his own bakery, but he wants to return to New York. He just doesn't make enough. I know many people who return to Ecuador, spend all the money they earned here in a very short time, and then come back to start again.

Things are as expensive as they are here. A pound of peas costs the same, but your income is only a fraction. If you make twenty dollars a day in Ecuador, you're considered to be doing well. But since everything is expensive, the money is immediately gone. That's one of the reasons why people don't want to work anymore. They even leave school, because why study? They won't do anything with it anyway. I know a lot of young people who came here because of all that.

I'm still working on my legal status. Five years ago, I applied for the US visa. It's the only way to legalize myself, and I'm still waiting. But I'm paying taxes. Since I got here, since day one, I paid taxes. And good that I did, because now I won't have problems with that. I have my Social [Security number] and the permission to work; I'm just waiting for the US visa so they can give me the green card one day. Because of the pandemic, it all took longer, and hopefully, I get it all done before it's too late. Because year after year I'm thinking, maybe next year I will go and see my parents, maybe next year, maybe next, and now it's twenty-three years since I left, and I'm desperate to see them because, you know, one day they will die. It's really eating me from inside. But I always know I left for a reason, and I'm here for a reason. I have my four beautiful kids; they are my life.

When I was fifteen, I wanted to go to the army and become a captain one day and maybe I would have—who knows. I still feel pain for having left my home and my family, maybe more than ever. My youngest brother was two years old when I left him—now he is here, and he is twenty-six. I met him as an adult, and every time I see him, I want to cry, because I think of all those missed years of seeing him growing up, of being with him.

My parents have a tomato farm now. Every time I talk to them, I thank them for the things they taught me as a kid. They showed me basically everything in that short time I had with them. All I achieved here I achieved because of them, especially my mother. My mother is my source of power. Whatever I do, I always ask myself what my mother will think about it. I want her to be proud of me, and I hope she is.

ANNA MARIE

'm from Ireland and the oldest of eleven children. Until I was eight, we lived in the town of Loughrea, which has a population of around five thousand people. Then we moved four miles up the road to a village called Newtowndaly. This is all on the western coast of Ireland, in Galway County.

The village was about a quarter mile stretch of road. It had ten houses. We didn't have house numbers or a zip code. When somebody wrote us a letter, they just put "Newtowndaly." We didn't have sidewalks or streetlamps, either. It was country, rural living. And we were the "town kids!" Even though the town we came from would be considered a village by New York standards, and it was just four miles away, for the few people in Newtowndaly, we were "townies." (*Laughs.*)

Most weekends I spent with our grandmother in our family shop, which had been opened in 1908. My grandmother ran it with my father. My family closed it in 2017. I was just there; I came back from Ireland ten days ago, which is why I remember everything about that time so vividly. And while I was rummaging around the old neighborhood, I was at the house where the shop used to be and found a sign that said "Patrick Lyons, Wool Merchant, Auctioneer, and General Merchant." That was my father. That was our shop.

It was a place of community in so many ways. It had everything—hardware, paint, timber, cement, gas, meat, groceries, fertilizer, and animal feed. It was a real country shop. And opposite the shop was my grandmother's house, a whitewashed two-story stone house with a red door and a thatched roof. It had one room upstairs—that was my grandmother's. The house did not have a toilet or running water, so my grandmother had a pot under her bed all the time—even fourteen years later when she lived with us! (*Laughs.*) But it was common in those times for people's houses not to have running water or toilets. My friend next door, they didn't have a toilet or running water until well into the '80s.

Her mother had five sons and one daughter, who was my friend. And her brothers were all out working—and every single one of them had a clean shirt on every day! I know this because my friend, who was my age, ironed every single one of those shirts. Always. I remember one weekend she ironed sixty-three shirts. Those shirts would be washed in a twin tub where you had to pour the water into it. You'd pull it out into the backyard, and that was all her job, and if we were around, we would all help or chat with her and listen to country music on the radio.

The privilege of living in my house was that we had a washing machine, and we had a dryer. Most people didn't have a dryer. The only reason we had a dryer was that my father, one time, was an auctioneer for a house that was being sold, and it had a dryer in it, an American tumble dryer, but nobody bought it, so he bought it and took it home. But because of the price of electricity, we never used it much. We still don't use a dryer. When I was home two weeks ago, I hung sheets out on the line and later took them in.

But back to my grandmother's house. She used to render lamb fat in the oven to make lard; she called it "drippings." And that's what she would dress the carrots or the cabbage with when she was cooking vegetables. Oh, and we used to get up to devilment in that house. For example, we smoked as young kids, eight, nine years old, stealing cigarettes from my aunts, my father's sisters, who also lived in that house. (*Laughs.*) Oh, poor aunts . . . Sometimes we would take their high-heeled boots and go down to the fields in them, just to try them out, and of course, they got all covered in muck and dirt, and I'm sure we didn't think to clean them because, well, we had just borrowed them, no? (*Laughs.*)

My grandmother lost her husband at the age of fifty-one; he fell down the stairs and had a heart attack. So, she had to run a business and raise seven children at the same time. Her neighbor, Mrs. Clarke, also lost her husband at a young age. These two women used to visit each other's houses every night; they lived next door to each other and took up smoking cigarettes when their husbands died. They'd only smoke at night, but they'd go to each other's houses, and that continued until Mrs. Clarke died well into her nineties. However, my grandmother, who had dementia, would still go to the Clarkes' house and sit by the fire, trying to smoke a cigarette until she became bedridden at about eighty-eight. The Clarkes would always allow her to sit there by the fire, even though Mrs. Clarke was dead. In her dementia, my grandmother would say, "Where's Mrs. Clarke?" and whoever was there would answer, "Well, you know, Granny, Mrs. Clarke is dead." "What?" she would say. "Nobody told me that."

I just realized everyone knew my grandmother as "Granny." And my father was always known as "Dada," even out and about in public. "Oh, Dada. Where's Dada?" And still to this day—he's eighty-two—he's known as Dada for many, not Mr. Lyons.

At the shop, there were a lot of people working. You'd have two shopgirls, a guy in the yard, a guy in the hardware, and two people in the office doing the books—it was a thriving hive in its time. And those six people got their dinner served; it was included in their payment, except once a week they would go to town for their Friday lunch. Sometimes the girls would take me with them; I was still a child, and I would have beans and chips and fish or something, and it was such a treat for me. Those are the things I remember.

That shop provided quite a sense of community. People would come for all kinds of things; the shop was a country shop, [and a] post office, and we paid out pensions, and often they came just for a chat. As the oldest of eleven siblings, I started helping in our shop when I was nine or ten years old. My father taught me a lot there. His motto was: "If anything is worth doing, it's worth doing well." My mother worked there too, but she wasn't well-liked because she was a townie and, well . . . It took the local people a long time to accept my mother because she could be a bit judgy and a bit . . . I don't know. An example: A neighbor would come up seven days a week to our shop, and she'd see the bread truck passing, so she'd know the bread was fresh. But she'd come into the shop feeling all the bread—"Is that fresh, Mary? And this one, is that fresh?"—while the steam was still rising from those breads! So, yes, they were fresh. But also, all these breads were sliced, and by touching them, the lady kind of ruined them for the next person. So, my mother would say, "What are you doing?" She was calling it out, and you can do that; these are country folk, they are not easy to upset. It was just the way she did it, her tone, I guess.

A better example: There was a woman, Breda Flynn. She would come to the shop once a week to get her pension, and she would always want a half pound of sausages. There were two kinds of sausages we got delivered: one was in packets wrapped, and the others were loose. So, the loose sausages, it's easier to give you a half pound, but Breda Flynn wouldn't want those. She didn't like them. You'd have to cut the packet for her. That used to annoy my mother. My father and I were like, "It doesn't matter. We're selling sausages, you know." So, Mrs. Flynn would love to see us there because we would give her what she wanted. Plus, we were eleven kids—if we don't sell the sausages, we'll take them home and eat them. They wouldn't get wasted.

I firmly believe that the Breda Flynns of the world and working in that shop taught me hospitality and allowed me to work in restaurants today. People just want to be met where they're at. And Breda Flynn likes to be fussed over. I'm not here to teach her manners. I'm here to take her money. Realistically, as much of it as I can get. But in a nice way, you know? Breda is going to buy the sausages either way. So let her feel important about how she's buying them. I learned that from my father. He would charm the birds out of the trees for the Breda Flynns of the world. And so she came to buy a half pound of sausages, and she'd leave with a leg of mutton. Because my father would say, "OK, Breda. God, you're awfully fussy about your sausages. But we'll do that for you, Breda. Now, have a lovely leg of lamb in here. It's a small one. This'll be great for soup during the week, Breda." She would spend more, and all you had to do was give her the half pound of sausage just the way she wanted it, you know?

Then you had Mrs. Healy, whom I saw just two weeks ago. I went for a walk down an old road, a road I haven't been on in a long time, and I went by myself. This was just two weeks ago. What day is it today? Friday. Exactly two weeks ago, I went for this walk. There were a lot of new houses and such. So, I walked by. I knew where I was, but I didn't know whose house was whose anymore. So, I walked by, and there was a guy outside fixing his garden, and I looked at him and thought, "Oh, he's one of the Healys. I just don't know which one he is." So, I chanced it. I said, "Albert?" And he said, "No, it's Brian." And I was like, "Oh, Brian, hi, how are you?" I said, "I'm Anna Marie. I don't know if you remember me." And he's like, "Oh, you're the oldest of the Lyonses." And I said, "I am." And then my daughter Kate, who was coming for a run and knew where I was walking, passed by, and I stopped her. I said, "Hey, come and meet Brian Healy. You've often heard me tell the story about Mrs. Healy, who used to come to the shop on her bicycle two to three times a week."

Mrs. Healy had eight children and was around the same age as my mother. She would come up to the store on her bicycle, rain, wind, or snow. We wouldn't have much snow, though. But when telling the story, you'd always throw in a bit of snow. (*Laughs.*) So, on her bicycle! She'd have two bags. In those bags, she'd have wrapped in newspaper up to forty eggs. So twice a week, she would bring the eggs to the shop, and we'd be delighted to see her coming because we would have forty farm eggs to sell. To Breda Flynn, for example, who would buy eggs because she couldn't keep hens anymore. So, you'd buy the eggs for ten pence, give her the four pounds, and then Mrs. Healy would buy groceries, and you'd get the four pounds back. I told that story many times at home, and now Kate was there, my daughter, and I said, "Look, this is Mrs. Healy's son! And you know in our dining room, the six steak knives, they're a brand called Newbridge and have a brown handle on them? It was this man's mother who gave me those six steak knives." And then I said to him, to Brian Healy, right then and there: "And that's why I often think of your mother."

To be fair, I wasn't sure where his mother was today, if she was still alive. But then he said, "Well, she's up there in the house. Would you like to say hello?" Of course, I wanted to! So, I went up and knocked on the door, and Mrs. Healy came to the door, just fourteen days ago! And you want to know what? She looks fantastic. She's probably about ninety-two and looks fantastic! I haven't seen her in probably twenty years.

So, we talked a little bit about her coming to the store on her bike, selling her forty eggs, and returning to her eight kids with groceries. She said, "I have such great memories of the shop and of your mother." And that's when I realized that I wasn't aware of the impact my mother had on people. Even though she wasn't loved in the beginning, she wound up really immersing herself in that world and community. Later in life, she learned the value of kindness and was better at it. And that day, Mrs. Healy told me a story that I didn't know. She said, "Your mother always gave me a box of chocolates and a card for Christmas." And I didn't know that. And she said, "And now your brother does the same." I didn't know that either. So, it continues a little bit.

My mother ended up working in the shop for probably the best part of thirty years, and I also spent a lot of time there. There were days that were slow. Maybe on a Monday evening, I would be making a pot of tea, and then someone like Dermot Murphy might come in to buy his newspaper and two packs of cigarettes for his wife. I would ask, "Sean, do you want a cup of tea?" To which he would reply, "Oh, I'll have a cup of tea." So, people would have cups of tea while standing in the shop. People would smoke in the shop, and maybe even have a beer, because when my grandmother was running it, she'd sell Guinness under the counter because, you know, people would want a bottle of Guinness here and there, and the shop didn't have a liquor license. So, there would often be people standing around chatting—farmers, men, women, all chatting. They could be talking about politics, for example.

There were two main parties in Ireland, both center-right: Fianna Fáil and Fine Gael. All the country people in our neighborhood were pretty much Fine Gael supporters. We were Fianna Fáil supporters, which back in the day would have been the old IRA—not the IRA there is today, but the people who formed it, like Michael Collins. My grandmother had a cousin on the run; he was involved in the first Dáil and the Irish Civil War of 1922. So, our political affiliations would have come from, you know, the Irish Republican Army. Prominent figures like Éamon de Valera, the front-runners of our policies, aimed to secure Ireland's liberation from English rule and establish a unified Irish nation.

My grandmother often told us the story of the Black and Tans, who were English soldiers sent to Ireland during the Irish War of Independence to help maintain British control. She told us how, when she was a child and lived with her sister at her aunt's house, who raised them, one night the Black and Tans arrived. They were taken out of their house, and petrol was poured around it. "But," my grandmother used to say, "not all the Black and Tans were bad," because there was this one guy who said, "Guys, this is a woman and two girls, two children. What are we doing? This is terrible!" And so, they didn't burn the house down and left. "And off we went," Granny used to say, laughing, "to sleep on our bed of guns." Because her aunt's house was a safe house for the IRA, and they were literally sleeping on beds of guns.

There were many stories like this one, and they all would be part of how I grew up. Our house had always been busy, and there were always people coming and going and telling stories, and in the shop too. And then my grandmother moved in with us when we moved out to the country when I was eight. And that house that I described, and that I walked the ruins of the other day, was neglected because it was too expensive to get it thatched in the 1980s. So the house was knocked to the ground. It was probably there for about 150 years, and if we had known then what we know now about how to rebuild things . . .

The Ireland of the 1970s and 1980s was a country about moving forward so much because they had stood still for so long. Nobody saw the value in the old. And they were building modern houses and bungalows and things were being knocked down left, right, and center. It's almost only in the last twenty years that they're realizing, "Oh, wait a minute, we should have kept some of these things." Like, our village was dotted with thatched houses, you know. And people who had the skill to thatch were becoming rarer and rarer. And then it was becoming just too expensive and nobody cared because Ireland was so moving forward.

My mother came to visit me here in New York in 1993. It was her first time to visit, and she couldn't get over what she felt was such a desire in New York to hang on to the old. She was born in 1944, and she was what we call a post–World War II baby. She grew up with rations. And Ireland in the 1950s, you know, if you think about Frank McCourt's book *Angela's Ashes*, that was all real. And it hadn't moved much forward until the 1960s or 1970s. So, there was such a drive to move forward that people didn't really care to preserve the old stuff. Well, that house, our house, is gone, is what I'm trying to say.

So, Granny lives with us in that house, right? So, that house now has eleven children, a grandmother, a mother, a father—and then we had Molly Flynn. After the ninth child was born, Divinia, my mother needed help in the house. So, Molly Flynn, who had worked in my father's family's house when he was a young man, now came to work for us from Monday to Friday. She made brown bread, cooked dinners, and cleaned the house. Molly became like a grandmother to us.

And then there was a fellow by the name of Sean McFadden. When my mother was forty, Sean was sixty. Sean McFadden had moved in with his sister to help her raise her children, and when the children got old enough, the rumor was that the oldest son kicked him out. But Sean never let anybody know that. Instead, he used to live in a shed up the road from where his sister's house was. He had a bicycle and all his belongings in the shed. One of my friends tried to follow him home one night to see, but Sean's routine was, on his bicycle, he'd stop into Kennedys', which was our neighbor's. Sometimes he'd shave out in the backyard there. Sometimes he would shave in the backyard of our house. He would do odd jobs. He was a handyman. He always wore a suit and a peaked cap, shining. His shoes were shining too, and his hair was always lacquered, real cream. And he would come to our house, and he'd . . . Well, there was no real agreement about doing work. But my mother knew Sean, and my father would explain to us if we asked: "Well, this is Sean McFadden; he helps with things." If there was wood to be chopped, he'd chop it. If there was a fire to be lit, he would light it. Him and Molly Flynn knew each other, and she would say, "Sean, would you help me with this? Sean, would you help with that?" Before Molly started working for us, and while my mother was pregnant once more, Sean would come to the house. My mother was heavily pregnant, but she still had to cook dinner for my father and whoever was working in the shop. So, to be ready by one, Sean would arrive around eleven. He'd start cleaning the vegetables, washing dishes, helping out. "Lie down now, Missus." And then Sean would call her around twenty minutes to one, twenty minutes before my grandmother and my father would be up for dinner. Sean had never let on that he was the one cooking the dinner. My mother would just get his secret help; it was their little thing. He was helping her out because she was so tired. She'd take a nap, he would help, and later she'd buy him twenty cigarettes, or she might slip him a twenty at some point.

He used to smoke Sweet Afton, non-filtered cigarettes. And then he and Molly were friends, and they'd go dancing at local dances. Tommy always rode his bicycle, and he always whistled. When you were making hay, he'd be there to help; if you were making silage, he'd help with that. He helped everyone in the village. At the age of sixty-nine, Sean met a woman, got married, and moved to the city of Galway. We were like, "What?" And then he died two years later, and everyone was so sad because finally, Sean, who had been homeless in a very rural way for probably ten or fifteen years, finally had found some comfort, and then he died at seventy-one. He was a part of our household. We treated him with respect. There might have been times he babysat us, if there was such a thing. There were often times my parents would be gone, but Sean would be there. It was just that kind of place. Our house was that kind of place. Our village was that kind of place.

Houses were just a community, if you like. We would go to Kennedys' in summertime to play cards. The Kennedys had five boys and a girl, so all the boys' friends would come to play cards, and we'd go there to play cards too. We learned to play Progressive Twenty-five. There's a game called Twenty-five. You play with partners, and you can play in threes—a game of strategy. We played for money, you know, like fifty pence. The old people would join, the young people would join, Gertie Kennedy would make us cups of tea and sandwiches, and John Kennedy would tell us stories about the old *piseogs*. It's Gaelic and means traditional Irish folk beliefs and superstitions; you don't know if they're true or not true. Stories people tell each other. This is a derivative of back in the day in Ireland, when *seanchaís*, storytellers, would go house to house. In our time, John Kennedy would tell us these stories, and we loved hearing them.

Stories of ghosts or sightings and so on. It was John Kennedy who taught me what happens if you meet a dead person. John would say, "You need to be more afraid of the people that are living than the people that are dead." And I'd be like, "John, what do you do if you meet a dead person?" "The first thing you do," he would say, "is bless yourself and ask them if you can help them. I'm just sharing that with you in case, okay?" So, lots of stories of banshees. Three knocks to a door! (*Knocks on the table three times.*) My friend Darina Flanagan would tell me the night her father died, she heard a knock at the door. My mother was very curious about things like that and asked a lot about it. My mother loved history, loved tracing families, and learning about that sort of stuff. That was one of the things that Mrs. Healy reminded me of. She said my mother knew everything about local history, and she would talk to people, and that was how she wound up being fondly remembered because she didn't discount country people.

A banshee is like a mermaid, but she's not a mermaid. She has long hair. Sadie Byrne would swear she hears the banshee. She was our local hairdresser. You'd go get your hair done, and she'd be like, "Did you hear the banshee?" "No, Sadie, we didn't hear the banshee." And she'd be like, "Did you hear of anyone dead? I could have sworn I heard the banshee the other night." The thing was, there was always somebody dying, so you'd hear somebody was dead, and you'd be like, "Oh, Sadie was right."

The same house today, Sadie's house, where we used to go get our hair done—a *piseog* would be that you never knocked down a single hawthorn bush in a field because that's a fairy fort. And it's bad luck on your house or in your family if you knock down a lone hawthorn bush in a field. So, they built their landscaping or their front lawn around this hawthorn bush not to tear it down because you would respect this kind of *piseog*. So that's part of where I came from.

Now, the beauty of all of that is that everybody knows everybody. And that's also some of the annoying parts of it. You couldn't go anywhere without being known. Everybody would know, "That's Pat Lyons's daughter." You couldn't get into much trouble because you'd be reported back. And people loved to gossip and chat. So, as I was becoming older, I didn't want to be known as my father's daughter. I wanted to be known as myself. I don't know where that came from.

So, when I finished high school, or the Irish equivalent to that, I wanted to go out and work. My parents said, "No, you're going to go to college or university." It wasn't trendy at the time; it was starting to become so, and now, of course, it's natural that everybody goes to college. But at the time, not everybody did it. In fact, two of my best friends didn't. They're still in the jobs they learned back then. I met one of them two weeks ago, and I asked her, "How long have you been at Omak?" And she said, "I've been there for thirty-four years." Anyway, back then, I wanted to go get a job. My father was like, "No, you're going to go to college. It'll be the best three or four years of your life." But when you're seventeen, three or four years seem like an eternity. I remember being appalled and angry that he would think I would want to do something like that for three or four years.

To make a long story short, I went. And I could not believe how my mind was completely blown open to a whole new set of people and ideas. Not all churches had women sit on one side of the church and men sit on the other! Other people had different ideas about things, and all that was a whole new experience for me! I'm grateful for my parents. They weren't as narrow-minded as some of the people growing up in the country were. But they certainly weren't as open-minded as this whole new bunch of people I was meeting at eighteen years of age.

I didn't even realize until quite recently that my mother really was the homemaker. The husband had the final say. For a woman who raised seven daughters, and all seven daughters are mighty women, she was very traditional. I remember her one time saying to me that she thinks it's harder for me now, for us women now, because we have to go out and get jobs. In her time, you didn't have to do that. You got married, and you had your children, and your husband was paramount. In our house, my father always got the best cut of meat. He always got served first. For his teatime, he could have lamb chops and beans and whatever you'd have, and we might have boiled eggs on toast. It was very much the man, the man, the man.

I called my mother after Donald Trump was elected, and I said, "We're all devastated here." She says, "What do you mean you're devastated?" She said, "Who else did you think would win?" This was when he ran against Hillary Clinton. And I said, "Well, I thought it would be Hillary." My mother said without hesitation, "That's no job for a woman." I couldn't believe it. That was the first time I realized it . . . I mean, Mother, you have raised general managers for women! You have a nurse, you have a daughter with a PhD in chemistry, you have a teacher, you have a barrister and a quality engineer. Your sons, on the other hand, as much as I love my brothers, are nowhere near as academically successful or independent as their sisters. I don't know what happened. It's for another discussion. It's fascinating. So, anyhow, fast-forward.

I got it into my head: I wanted my own independence. College helped me with that—and was an avenue to go further. Three years later I went to the States, just for the summer, or so I thought. I never thought I would be in the States forever. I always thought I'd come home and live my life there. But there was a love interest back home that didn't work out. So I said, I'll stay. I was twenty then. I was legal for four months—I had come on a J-1 visa—and then I stayed for another year and a half, illegally, and I was terrified. Terrified!

When I finally applied for my new visa, which was a lottery visa, I said to myself, "If I'm meant to be here, I'll get it. And if I'm not meant to be here, I'll just stay for another little while and then I'll go home." Then I got it, and I was like, "OK, great, I'll stay." I had wound up being at home for six months in the process of getting this visa, and when I left that time, it was sadder than any time I had left before because this time I didn't know when I was coming back. And that was the start. When I came back to New York that time, I stayed here for three years without going home.

I came back [to the United States] to two of the summer jobs I had had. One was babysitting, and the other was working for a guy I had been housecleaning for in my first summer here. I worked for him for ten years, on and off, housecleaning and more. Even when I worked as a restaurant manager at BR Guest, sometimes I would clean for him on my two days off. He had an apartment in the city as well as out in the Hamptons, and sometimes he'd call me: "Oh my God, the place is a mess, you have to come out." So even on my two days off, I would go out to East Hampton and clean his house. I learned so much from him. I learned about culture. I had my first steak tartare at his house because he was a great home cook.

He's the reason I work in restaurants. First, back in 1990—I've been in this country for thirty-three years now—I was just a house cleaner for him in the city and out in East Hampton. Then he was moving to East Hampton full-time, so he asked me if I'd pack up his house. So I packed up his house and moved him out to East Hampton, and for a time I actually lived in his house on Park Avenue, on 96th Street, packing up his life four days a week. I would get up in the morning and cook breakfast for him, which was freshly squeezed orange juice and cinnamon toast, Arnold Pepperidge Farm bread. I would have his newspaper, and I would leave it outside his room at eight. And then I would start packing up or cleaning.

I learned about china. I learned about antiques. He had a lot of Staffordshire. You can buy this at fairs and carnivals, and it's more valuable if it doesn't have a marking on the back. He had Limoges china, so he explained that to me. He taught me how to set a table too. He taught me etiquette, I suppose, in some ways, just because I would work, and then at the end of the day, if he wasn't going to dinner, he was going to cook, so did I want to eat? Of course, that's how I had my first lobster. So, I learned how to eat lobster. I learned how to cook frozen peas to make them taste like fresh peas. Steak tartare—he got a great kick out of cooking that for me because he knew I was Irish, and we eat everything medium-well. He taught me the basics of wine and things like that.

I fell into place there in a weird way. His wife was dead before I ever got to this country. She had only died maybe a couple of years beforehand, but in their house in East Hampton I could really feel her presence, maybe because I grew up with all these stories. I almost felt like I knew this woman, and he would tell wonderful things about her. His heart was broken, but he recovered nicely and was able to start dating younger women as time moved on, much to his daughter's dismay. But anyhow, I digress.

So, we packed up the house on Park Avenue and moved out to East Hampton. I wasn't supposed to stay out there, but he said, "Oh, you have to help me unpack now." He was very controlling about where he wanted things and how he wanted them done. Then he had to go to the city for three days after this first move. So he went, and he didn't give me much direction. When he came back, I pretty much had everything sorted. I had put his house and kitchen in order the way it was organized on Park Avenue. All the spices were going to be right here and so on, so his movements were the same in the kitchen. And he was like, "Oh, my God!" After that, he only made suggestions to me. We spent four months figuring out the house, setting it all up. There were things that needed to be cleaned out, things in the attic, and others. A life, I suppose, somebody else's life. We cataloged it all and put it back together.

I made a map of where things were, and he had it for years. I often went to see him afterward, like ten, fifteen, twenty years later, and he still had that road map of how the attic was laid out, so that he could find anything he was looking for. I learned from him to buy wine and water glasses from Crate and Barrel by the case. You buy them in bulk, and then you don't notice how much you break at a time, you know? And he was the one who suggested that I work in restaurants. Well, no, sorry. He wanted me to go to Cornell to learn hotel and restaurant management. And he was going to pay for that, and then I would have to pay him back. I was like, "All right, hell, no." I knew the last time I went to college worked out, but I was not doing this again. So, we set me up for an interview with a friend of his at the Fraunces Tavern over in the South Street Seaport.

I dressed up for that interview and paid $400 for a suit. I don't think I've paid $400 for a suit since. So I went to the interview, but the guy wasn't even there. I met his wife, who apparently hated him; she pawned me off to an Irish waiter. The waiter said, "Do you like working?" I said, "I have a guy that I work for—he thinks I should go into restaurant or hotel management." The waiter said, "Have you ever worked in a restaurant?" My inner dialogue is, *I don't even eat out. I don't even know what you're talking about.* He says, "Why don't you get a job working in a restaurant first?" I said, "Sure, give me a number." He said, "Go over to South Street Seaport. There is a guy who owns a restaurant named Harbor Lights—he's from Galway, I think. See what he says." I couldn't wait to get out of there.

It was June 11th, 1993. It was my friend's birthday, and I was in charge of getting the cake, so I decided not to go to South Street Seaport. I walked up Fulton Street, put my foot down on the subway to catch the 7 train to go home to Queens. But then I told myself, that guy was so nice to me, I should at least do what he said. I turned on my heels and went back down to the Seaport, went to the place he had told me to. And there, the guy at the door turned me away.

You know, I was this twenty-three-year-old eager beaver, bright-eyed and bushy-tailed. And the guy was like, "Have you worked in restaurants?" I said no, and off he sent me. But the owner of that restaurant, his name is Austin Delaney, was at his table nearby and probably heard my accent. He stood up, came to the door and said, "What's your name?" "My name is Anna Marie." "Oh, same name as my daughter. What's going on?" "Well, I'm looking for a job." "Come in and sit down." So, I sat at this table, which I later learned was table nine. It was where he had lunch with all his cronies—a sailor that he used to take care of and who'd come up for lunch every day, a businessperson, and the people that worked for him. They'd all have lunch every day at table nine. I sat there for an hour telling my story. When I was done, he said, "I have to go downstairs and back a horse; I'll be right back."

I didn't know that "going downstairs" meant to cross the street, to go to Water Street and to the OTB [off-track betting], where he would put a bet on a horse. He owned horses, and one of his horses was running. He didn't come back for about three hours. The bartender, whose name is Bill Kenny, a man in his sixties, a walking pickle because he drank so much, but he was amazing, was from Tuan, which is in County Galway as well, but a different part of County Galway—well, he kind of took care of me for the afternoon. I sat at the bar, drinking Diet Coke, and then about five o'clock I was like, "That's it, I'm having a beer." I met so many people that day. I came home and I said to my friends, "If we ever need to get a job in an office, we need to go to a restaurant or a bar on a Friday evening dressed to the nines." I was up and down the bar chatting with people, and I just had the best time; I didn't care if I ever got a job.

Meanwhile, Mr. Hirsch—my mentor, if you will—was at home in East Hampton waiting to find out how the interview went. So, when I called him, I had had three or four bottles of beer and not eaten all day, so I was full of the joys of life! (*Laughs.*) Long story short: The owner finally came back that evening and said, "I don't know if we have a job for you, but we'll train you anyway." So, they did. I worked there for five years. I waited tables there, at Harbor Lights—it was the best time. I met the best of friends. I still have them today. I don't see them that often, obviously, but definitely three of them are still in my life. And there are others that I know I can pick back up anytime.

Anyhow, you get a little burnt out waiting tables—you get a little snippy. I became that waitress who was like, you know . . . I remember one day somebody asking me, "Could you pour me water?" And I was like, "I only have two hands, I'll be right back." So, I stepped out, started working in an office, a medical office, doing medical billing. Then I worked somewhere else doing reception. And I remember being up in Harlem, it was on 128th Street, it was a beautiful day, and I was looking out, thinking, "I wonder what they're doing at Harbor Lights today." Next moment I pick up the phone and I say, "I want to come back." And they're like, "OK."

I worked five doubles, Monday to Friday, for about two and a half years. What I knew was, I loved the restaurant business. And I said to myself, "Well, if I'm going to do this, I may as well do it right." So, I decided to quit and go looking for a managing job. I had no management experience, no other job, and no idea what else to do. By the second week of February, I started working for BR Guest at the Ocean Grill. And all the things that came before now applied. I was here to take care of people, not to teach manners. I was here to be kind to people and have things ready for them—in one of the finest restaurants in New York.

One of the things I love about New York is the diversity. I don't know what would have happened if I had stayed in Ireland. I have some sisters who are quite conservative. But I've now been here longer than I was there. I'm very glad for where I came from. I'm very grateful for the upbringing I had. But I am extremely grateful that I live here now.

I remember my mother one time saying to me, "I'm a Catholic, and you were raised Catholic, but please don't have eleven children." I said, "Don't worry, Mother, I won't."

Growing up with eleven children, we didn't notice the difference, but I did notice that it was almost like two families for her. There were the older ones and the younger ones. What applied to the first four or five of us didn't apply to the last five or six of us. That's also interesting because I was born in 1969 and grew up in the '70s when our parents were kind of flush. The business went into liquidation in the '80s, and they had to buy everything back to hold on to what they had. So, my younger sisters—nine, ten, and eleven, the last three—they had a different upbringing than me. They came home to an empty house because we didn't have Molly Flynn anymore. We couldn't afford it. So, they would often come home from school at five in the evening; cold, wet, wintery evenings. They'd come home and they'd have to put on a fire. They'd have to cook their own dinner. They might even have to go down to the shop to get things for their dinner.

Things were tighter. The businesses weren't doing well. Ireland was changing. People weren't coming to the shops selling eggs anymore. The health sanctions that were put into local businesses because of the European Union made things very difficult. My mother would get sick when she would hear the health department was coming. They would give her all these citations and things you'd have to spend money on fixing. It had operated like this for 150 years, and now you couldn't sell eggs anymore. So, things changed, and my younger brothers and sisters had a different upbringing than me. Maybe that was my privilege, that I had it better. It was still hard work and it was all the things it was, but it was different. For me, there was always dinner and a fire when I came home from school. I feel that I have lived many lives.

ACKNOWLEDGMENTS

My involvement with this book has been one of the most meaningful endeavors of my career. The book began as a vague idea to somehow recognize those who have contributed to the success that restaurants have enjoyed in this country. I was not certain how to proceed even after I had completed six or seven interviews. The book took a more realistic turn while I was driving down a bumpy dirt road in Chiapas, Mexico, with friends Tino Hanekamp and his wife, Ixtzel Arreola. Tino stopped suddenly as I began to describe this imprecise idea of interviewing current and former employees. Tino's enthusiasm for the project carried me through the process of development. Without his skilled transcription, advice, and constant help, this book would not have been realized.

A special thanks must be given to my literary agent, William Clark, who persisted, unfazed by the various rejections. I am also particularly grateful to Catherine Tung, my editor at Beacon Press, who was passionate about adding *Voices from the Kitchen* to a distinct oral history category at Beacon.

And, finally, with boundless appreciation, to the person who changed my life—my love, my wife, Victoria Freeman, who has always believed in me. Also, I would be incomplete without my sons, Rolan and Marlon. Rolan and my wonderful daughter-in-law, Sara, have brought enchantment and joy with grandchildren Elio and Rami. What more is there to ask for?

01 14